ARBITRATION FOR CONTRACTORS

Douglas A. Stephenson
BSc, CEng, FICE, FIStructE, FCIArb

Consulting Civil and Structural Engineer
Member of Council, Chartered Institute of Arbitrators

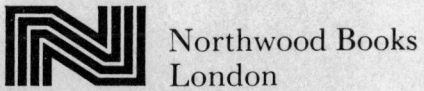

Northwood Books
London

Published 1982

© Douglas Stephenson and Northwood Publications 1982

ISBN 7198 2900 3

A 'Construction News' book

Printed and bound in Great Britain by Short Run Press Ltd, Exeter

Contents

Acknowledgements   iv

Foreword   v

Author's Preface   vii

1. Introduction   1
2. Arbitration Agreements   7
3. Powers of an Arbitrator   14
4. Appointment of the Arbitrator   18
5. Preliminaries   22
6. Evidence   33
7. The Hearing   38
8. The Award   43
9. Costs   51
10. Finality of the Award; Enforcement; Appeals   57
11. The Contractor as Claimant   62

Appendices:

A   Specimen Documents   77
B   The Arbitration Act 1950   107
C   The Arbitration Act 1975   131
D   The Arbitration Act 1979   135
E   The Arbitration Act 1979 (Commencement) Order 1979   144
F   Flow chart

Bibliography   145

Index   146

Acknowledgements

The author and publishers wish to acknowledge permission from the following to reproduce copyright material: Her Majesty's Stationery Office (Appendices B, C, D and E); The Institution of Civil Engineers (Form ArbICE).

Foreword
by Lord Justice Donaldson

If any justification is needed for this book, it is that arbitration is a 'mystery' in both senses of the word. It is a mystery in the sense of being a skilled craft, whether considered from the viewpoint of the arbitrator or from that of the disputant and those acting on his behalf. It is also a mystery in the sense of being a secret or hidden thing of which, lamentably, some arbitrators and many disputants are to a great extent ignorant.

Arbitration is a vitally important alternative to resorting to the Courts for the settlement of disputes. If it did not exist, it would have to be invented, because the Courts could not possibly handle the sheer volume of disputes which arise in a complex modern society. But, as is now generally recognised, it should be a real alternative, operating to the same standards as do the Courts, although not necessarily employing the same approach and procedures. Any contrast between the alternatives offered should not be between amateurism and professionalism, but between two brands of professionalism.

This being the case, arbitrators, like judges, have to learn their craft. So too do those who assist in the process by presenting the rival contentions of the parties. Experience will be the ultimate teacher under both systems, but experience will teach only slowly and may indeed mislead in the absence of basic knowledge acquired from books or teachers.

The procedures used in the arbitration of construction industry disputes are traditionally more akin to those adopted by the Courts than is the case with some other types of arbitration. But there is no need for those engaged in construction disputes to have a detailed knowledge of the whole range of law and Court procedures. In this book the author has been selective, and rightly so. The result is an invaluable guide of manageable proportions dealing with every relevant aspect of the craft.

I am honoured and delighted to have been asked to write a brief word of welcome to a book which, I know, will strip arbitration of its mysteriousness whilst supporting it as a mystery or craft.

Author's Preface

Although written primarily as a guide to the civil engineering contractor who finds himself involved in a dispute arising from a construction contract this book necessarily covers a wider field than that seen by one of the parties. For if arbitration is to serve its purpose as an inexpensive and expeditious means of resolving such disputes it must be properly understood and used; and understanding cannot be gained through a blinkered study from a single viewpoint. Accordingly the objective of this book is to provide an introduction to the practice of arbitration in general. I have however chosen examples relating to (imaginary) construction disputes.

A by-product of this more general approach to the subject is that the book will, I hope, be of value not only to contractors in the narrow sense of the word but also to employers, engineers and arbitrators in the field of construction, and to those who are contractors in the widest sense: namely that they are parties to a commercial contract.

Although arbitration has for many decades been the chosen method by which disputes arising from construction contracts are resolved, the manner of its use, and in particular the way in which arbitrators have been chosen, has until recently left much to be desired. It is only since the early 1970s that the need for arbitrators to know about arbitration has been recognised by the Institution of Civil Engineers; prior to this the principal, if not the sole, criterion was eminence as a civil engineer. Too often the arbitrator appointed was in the position of that person who is reputed, when asked if he could play the piano, to have replied: 'I don't know—I've never tried'.

Inevitably one consequence of this lack of understanding has been to turn for advice to lawyers, many of whom see arbitration as a poor substitute for legal action through the courts, with all of the disadvantages associated with such actions but none of the advantages. Arbitration has in this way gained a reputation for being anything but inexpensive and expeditious; and the procedure has been blamed for shortcomings for which the real blame lies with its users.

Much has been done by the Chartered Institute of Arbitrators to foster understanding and efficient use of the procedure, by means of training courses and by setting standards of proficiency as a prerequisite to appointment to panels from which arbitrators are selected when the Chartered Institute is the appointing authority.

My experience during the past few years as a tutor and more recently as a course director of certain of these training courses has proved of immense value in writing this book. In particular it has drawn attention to the difficulty encountered by many students in drafting the many letters and documents used in the proceedings, notwithstanding that these usually follow a standard format requiring little adaptation to suit a particular reference. Accordingly I have included, in Appendix A, a series of specimen letters and documents which, while not applicable to every situation, will in most cases provide at least a format and a basis for adaptation to a particular need.

The reasons underlying the choice of arbitration as the means whereby construction and other disputes are resolved are not hard to find. It is flexible, enabling it to be adapted to suit the needs of a particular dispute, large or small, simple or complex. It provides for determination by a person who understands the technicalities of the subject matter, and for the privacy and convenience of the parties. And properly used it should be both cheaper and quicker than litigation.

Where the parties, under the direction of a sensible arbitrator, behave sensibly, all of these objectives should be achieved. Where one party finds itself confronted by an obstructive or dilatory opponent it should bring such behaviour to the notice of the arbitrator with a request that it be taken into account in his award of costs. And where a party finds the arbitrator to be inexperienced it can lead him gently to adopt sensible procedures.

If this book helps in promoting the use of such procedures it will have served its purpose.

Being of an introductory nature this small volume does not attempt to deal with the complexities of the law or with procedural difficulties that sometimes arise during the course of a reference. For such matters 'Russell' and other major works are available and are listed in the bibliography. I have however attempted to explain in simple terms the significance of some

AUTHOR'S PREFACE

of the more important decisions of the courts affecting the conduct of arbitrations.

In writing the Foreword Lord Justice Donaldson, President of the Chartered Institute of Arbitrators, has bestowed upon this book an honour that I can only hope it deserves. He has also read through the typescript and given guidance on two matters of legal complexity, namely the law relating to the award of interest, and the powers available to an arbitrator, through the High Court, in dealing with reluctant or obstructive parties. For both of these actions, and for his encouragement, I am deeply grateful.

I am also indebted to my good friend and co-tutor Ian Menzies for his preliminary reading of the typescript and for making many helpful and constructive suggestions.

Douglas Stephenson
March 1982

1. Introduction

Synopsis
The basic principle of arbitration, namely that the parties to a contract from which a dispute arises elect to appoint a tribunal of their own choice to determine that dispute, is especially relevant where, as in construction, technicalities are involved. But arbitration depends for its efficacy upon the law: for without a framework of law within which recognition is given, the award of an arbitrator could prove worthless if the losing party chose to ignore it. Enforcement of arbitration awards is available to the parties through the courts of England and of most other civilised countries: though the law of England will in general require that the arbitration proceedings have been conducted, and the award made, in accordance with that law.

Definition
'An arbitrator is a private extraordinary judge between party and party, chosen by their mutual consent to determine controversies between them. And arbitrators are so called because they have an arbitrary power: for if they observe the submission and keep within due bounds, their sentences are definite from which there lies no appeal.'

The words of Lord Chief Justice Sir Robert Raymond, expressed some 250 years ago, still provide a valid definition: for if the phrase 'due bounds' is taken to mean 'the law', there is indeed no appeal from an arbitrator's award. The limited grounds upon which an appeal may lie only cover points of law, including failure by the arbitrator to conduct himself or the proceedings in accordance with the law (see Chapter 10).

Arbitration is a voluntary procedure, available as an alternative to litigation, but not enforcible as the means of settling disputes except where the parties have entered into an arbitration agreement. In such cases the right of either party to have disputes resolved by arbitration will, except where there are good reasons to the contrary, be upheld by the court (see p. 8).

Legal framework
This book is concerned with arbitration under English law, which applies in England and in Wales, but not in Scotland nor in Northern Ireland. English law applies automatically as the procedural law of arbitrations arising from contracts under the ICE Conditions, the FCEC Form of Subcontract, the JCT Forms of Contract or any other standard form where the contract is made and the work is to be performed in England or Wales, and where no other system of law is specified in the contract.

English law will also apply to arbitrations arising from contracts of a non-domestic type (that is, where one or both parties are based overseas, or where the work is to be performed overseas), where the parties elect that it shall apply. Their choice in this matter is not necessarily affected by their choice of the proper law of the contract (the law by which the contract is to be construed), although in general there will be a presumption to that effect where no other system of law is specified.

It is desirable that where English law governs the arbitration procedure the place of the arbitration should be within the jurisdiction of English courts so that the many 'supervisory' functions provided by those courts and described in this book are readily available.

There are indeed good reasons why arbitrations should be conducted under English law even in the case of non-domestic contracts, and even when the proper law of the contract is not English law. Firstly, English commercial law, and especially arbitration law, is more highly developed and sophisticated than any other legal system. Secondly, it forms the basis of many other legal systems throughout the world, and is therefore more readily accepted and understood than other systems. Thirdly, the general use of the English language in many overseas contracts reduces the problems of interpretation where English arbitration law is adopted.

English law of arbitration
Arbitration in England is known to have been recognised in common law since the beginning of the seventeenth century: indeed the system is claimed to be as old as legal history. The first statute was the Arbitration Act 1697, since which date there have been a number of re-enactments. Fortunately for today's practitioners, however, much of the law of arbitration was

summarised and codified in the Arbitration Act 1950 (referred to herein as the 1950 Act) and this Act, except for one major change, has remained substantially unaltered, being now referred to as the 'principal Act'.

The 1950 Act (see Appendix B) has the merits of simplicity and clarity. It also performs the valuable function of filling gaps that might otherwise exist in arbitration agreements, by defining the constitution of the tribunal, authorising the arbitrator to make orders, to make an award at any time, to make an interim award, to order specific performance and to award costs. But perhaps the most important function of the 1950 Act is that contained in Section 26 wherein an arbitration award may effectively be converted into a judgment of the High Court.

One of the main features of arbitration under English law is the emphasis laid upon compliance with the law. The danger has long been recognised that arbitrators, who are generally not qualified legally and who conduct proceedings in private, may stray from the law of the land, developing their own fund of 'case law' based upon their own concept of equity. In so doing they might well diverge from the law, not only as a body of arbitrators, but also as individuals; 'legal' precedents set by each individual might differ both from those of common law and from each other. In order to control this danger a system was set up, originally under the Common Law Procedure Act 1854 and more recently in the 1950 Act, whereby a point of law arising either during the course of a reference or in an award might, on the application of either party or of the arbitrator, be made the subject of a 'Special Case' for determination by the High Court.

Although this procedure, which was defined in Section 21 (later repealed) of the 1950 Act, provided a means by which case law developed to a high degree of sophistication in commercial contracts, it also provided a means whereby an unmeritorious party might delay the day of judgment. For by applying to the arbitrator for an award in the form of a special case on some spurious point of law, and then pursuing that point through the hierarchy of the courts, the losing party in an arbitration could delay, sometimes for many years, the date upon which payment became due, thereby gaining a financial advantage because of the unrealistically low rate of interest allowed in law upon arbitration awards.

Pressure from a number of commercial and legal bodies, and in particular from the Chartered Institute of Arbitrators, has resulted in the special case procedure being repealed, and replaced by a limited right of appeal on points of law, under Section 1 of the Arbitration Act 1979 (referred to herein as the 1979 Act; see Appendix D), which came into force on 1 August 1979 and applies to all arbitrations commenced after that date, and to other arbitration where it is adopted by agreement of the parties.

The 1979 Act makes provision, under Section 2, for a limited right to apply to the High Court for determination of a point of law arising in the course of a reference (see Chapter 13). It also fills certain gaps in the principal Act, such as that which arises when an appointing authority named in an arbitration agreement neglects or refuses to make the appointment, and it strengthens the power of an arbitrator to deal with a recalcitrant party.

In order to complete the list of statutes currently applicable to arbitration mention is also necessary of the Arbitration Act 1975 (Appendix C), the principal purpose of which is 'to give effect to the New York Convention on the Recognition and Enforcement of Foreign Arbitral Awards'. This Act is not, however, relevant to domestic arbitrations.

Advantages of arbitration

Many of the advantages most frequently claimed of arbitration as an alternative to litigation are especially relevant to those arising from construction contracts.

(a) FREEDOM IN CHOICE OF ARBITRATOR

The parties to an arbitration agreement are free to choose a suitable person to be arbitrator. Frequently disputes arising from construction contracts involve such questions as whether or not certain ground conditions should have been foreseen by the contractor; whether or not it was reasonable for the engineer or architect to issue drawings when he did, or to give the instructions he gave; or questions may involve the technicalities of the various standard methods of measurement. A proper understanding of these and many other points that may arise can only be gained by long experience in the construction industry—and preferably experience both in contracting and as the engineer under the contract. Hence it is desirable that the arbitrator should in such cases be an experienced engineer (or, where appropriate, architect or quantity surveyor): and this objective is usually best achieved by naming as the appointed authority the president of the appropriate professional body.

While it is recognised that technical expertise is available in litigation through the appointment of experts, there is a very real danger that a non-technical judge may be influenced more by the eloquence and powers of explanation and persuasion of the expert than by the technical merits of his evidence.

(b) FLEXIBILITY

Disputes arising from construction contracts may in some cases involve a few thousand— perhaps even a few hundred—pounds, or they may involve tens or hundreds of millions. They may involve questions of principle that will affect future contracts, or may (more commonly) be of a 'one-off' nature affecting only the contract from which the dispute arose. They may involve technical or legal issues or both: and the credibility of the witnesses to be called may or may not be in doubt. All of these factors affect the choice of procedure and the most appropriate form and level of representation— if any—of the parties. In arbitration the parties are free to determine these matters by agreement; and while neither party can dictate to the other where it is thought, for example, that costs are being incurred unnecessarily, the party may bring its contentions to the notice of the arbitrator and request that he take them into consideration in his award of costs.

(c) ECONOMY

Critics of arbitration often argue that costs in total are likely to exceed those incurred in litigation, because in the latter the judge is paid out of the public purse, while the arbitrator is not. While true, this is not usually a major factor in the total costs of the proceedings: the arbitrator's charges are often much less than those of the parties' solicitors and counsel. Furthermore where technical matters are involved it is likely that experts will be needed to present such matters to a judge, but not to a technically qualified arbitrator. Again, proceedings in court are likely to be more protracted, and hence more costly, than in arbitration.

Economy is not achieved automatically by use of arbitration rather than litigation, but it may be achieved where the parties act sensibly in choosing the form of the proceedings and of their representation. Where one party acts sensibly but the other does not, it is within the power of the arbitrator to award costs accordingly.

(d) EXPEDITION

It is especially important in construction disputes that unnecessary delay in their resolution should be avoided. Such disputes often involve voluminous documentary and oral evidence of details of progress, instructions, delaying factors and other matters. With the passage of time records may get lost or dispersed; memories fade; staff move on or die; defective work may become obscured or affected by alterations. Furthermore in some cases progress of the remaining work may be delayed pending resolution of a dispute, for example where a contractor encounters conditions which he had not foreseen and which he claims entitle him to reimbursement of extra costs under Clause 12 of the ICE Conditions. Generally arbitration, if properly used, provides the means of resolving a dispute with the minimum of delay.

(e) PRIVACY

Arbitration proceedings, unlike those in the courts, are not open to the press or to the public; only those persons involved in the proceedings are entitled to attend. It is of course open to the parties, by agreement, to allow others to be present, and they often do so where for example the arbitrator wishes a pupil to gain experience. Such attendance is normally on the condition that the confidentiality of the proceedings will be respected.

Usually the parties to construction disputes have no wish to publicise either the matters disclosed at the hearing or any other details of a reference; and frequently the damage to a previously harmonious relationship between two parties resulting from a dispute is more rapidly healed where there has been no publicity.

(f) FINALITY

One respect in which arbitration under English law differs from that under most other legal systems is in the emphasis given to the need for awards to comply with the law. This point has been the subject of much criticism and debate in recent years, it being argued against the English system that finality is more important than legality and that, having chosen their arbitrator, the parties should be content to accept his decision, whether strictly in accordance with legal precedent or not.

Until the 1979 Act became law parties were able on the flimsiest of pretexts to ensure that an award, when given, would not be final, **but** was capable of being challenged through the courts. Now, however, the right to appeal is strictly limited (see Chapter 10) and may in some circumstances be eliminated entirely.

2. Arbitration Agreements

Synopsis
The principal requirement of an arbitration agreement, in order that the arbitration may be governed by the 1950 and 1979 Acts, is that it shall be in writing. Hence the inclusion or reference to one of the standard forms of construction contract incorporating an arbitration clause, in a properly executed contract, provides a valid arbitration agreement.

Many necessary terms of an arbitration agreement are deemed by the 1950 Act to have been included unless there is specific provision to the contrary. But arbitration agreements may go much further in prescribing rules for the conduct of the arbitration and in certain circumstances for exclusion of rights of appeal.

Definition
'In this part of the Act, unless the context otherwise requires, the expression "arbitration agreement" means a written agreement to submit present or future differences to arbitration, whether an arbitrator is named therein or not' (1950 Act, Section 32).

It follows that there could be difficulty in establishing the existence of a valid arbitration agreement where the contract is an oral one, or where for example a written tender has been accepted orally.

Agreements to refer
Arbitration agreements made before a dispute arises, such as those incorporated in the ICE, FIDIC and JCT forms of contract and in the FCEC form of subcontract are often termed 'agreements to refer' because they

provide for the reference to arbitration of any dispute that may arise from the contract.

Ad hoc agreements

Where a dispute arises from a contract in which there is no arbitration agreement within the meaning of the 1950 Act it is open to the parties to enter into an 'ad hoc' arbitration agreement in respect of that dispute. In practice however it may be difficult to persuade the parties—or for one party to persuade the other—to enter into any form of agreement once a dispute has arisen.

Protection against court proceedings

Where a party to a valid arbitration agreement chooses to ignore that agreement and commences proceedings in court it is open to the other party, before delivering a defence or taking any other step in the proceedings, to apply to the court for a stay of the action under Section 4 of the 1950 Act. The applicant must satisfy the court that he is ready and willing to proceed in accordance with the arbitration agreement, and the court must also be satisfied that there is no sufficient reason why the matter should not be referred in accordance with the agreement. Although the power of the court to order a stay of the court action is discretionary it will usually be exercised where these conditions are satisfied.

Constitution of tribunal

Generally, and almost invariably in domestic construction contracts, the reference is to a single arbitrator. Such an intention need not however be defined in the arbitration agreement, because under Section 6 of the 1950 Act a provision to this effect is deemed to be included in every arbitration agreement unless some other mode of reference is provided.

Appointment procedure

Although it is desirable that the parties to an arbitration agreement should define the way in which the arbitrator (if not named in the agreement) is to be appointed, especially if it is their intention that he should be appropriately qualified to deal with the technicalities involved, failure to include such a definition is not fatal to the operation of the arbitration agreement. Section 10 of the 1950 Act provides a procedure for the appointment of an arbitrator by the High Court where the parties are unable to agree upon an appointment, and it also deals with vacancies that arise where the appointed arbitrator is incapable of acting, or refuses to act, or dies.

Until the 1979 Act became law there remained a situation in which deadlock could be reached because of a breakdown in the machinery for the appointment of the arbitrator. There was no provision under the 1950 Act for filling a vacancy where the appointing authority named in the arbitration agreement refused, or failed within the time specified, to make an appointment. This defect has been remedied under Section 6 of the 1979 Act, which amends Section 10 of the 1950 Act to enable the High Court to make an appointment in this situation.

Arbitration rules

It is open to the parties to include in either form of an arbitration agreement, or in an addendum thereto made either before or after a dispute has arisen, any rules for the conduct of the arbitration, provided that such rules are not unlawful or contrary to public policy. Standard rules are published by such bodies as the Chartered Institute of Arbitrators, the London Court of Arbitration, the United Nations Commission on International Trade Law (the 'UNCITRAL Rules') and other bodies, usually with the intention of defining time limits for the various stages in a reference and of providing additional powers to assist the arbitrator in his conduct of the reference.

Similarly the parties may adopt by agreement any lawful rules they themselves formulate. Matters that might well be covered in such rules, especially where the dispute involves a small sum or where the issues arising from it are of a technical rather than a legal nature, are limitation of the right to appoint counsel or solicitors as the parties' representatives, limitations as to the appointment of technical experts, and provision for the dispute to be determined on written evidence only, perhaps in conjunction with an inspection of the works in question.

Much benefit can often be gained by the parties from an agreement to adopt rules appropriate to the magnitude and nature of the dispute, as a means of minimising costs and expediting the resolution of the dispute. It may however be difficult to foresee, at the time of making an agreement to refer, the nature and magnitude of disputes likely to arise: if they were foreseeable they would be dealt with in the terms of the contract. Hence the parties may find a need to amend or supplement their arbitration agreement after a dispute has arisen, and at this stage the relationship between the parties is often not conducive to agreement of any kind. Nevertheless a party who finds his opponent obstructive to sensible rules of procedure should ensure that his proposals are clearly set out in a letter to the other party and brought to the notice of the arbitrator, with a request that they are taken into consideration in the arbitrator's award of costs.

Where it is agreed between the parties that a published set of rules shall apply it is important that there should be a definition of the relevant edition of such rules, in order to avoid the possibility of contention, and consequent delay. Such definition could either state the publication date of the edition that is to apply, or could specify that the relevant edition shall be that current at the date of the arbitration agreement or at the date of commencement of the arbitration.

Exclusion agreements

The 1979 Act, which introduces a new procedure for judicial review of points of law arising either from an award or during the course of a reference, also provides a limited right of the parties to exclude such review. An agreement for this purpose is appropriately termed an 'exclusion agreement', and in domestic contracts it is valid only if entered into after the commencement of the arbitration.

The ICE Conditions of Contract

The current (fifth) edition of the ICE Conditions of Contract, and earlier editions of the form, incorporates as Clause 66 an arbitration agreement within the meaning of the 1950 Act. Hence, provided that the form is signed by both parties or is referred to in a properly constituted contract (that is, one incorporating a valid offer and a valid acceptance), it will bring the arbitration within the scope of the 1950 Act. The clause also makes provision for the arbitrator to be appointed, failing agreement between the parties, by the President (or a Vice-President) of the Institution of Civil Engineers; and for the President to make, on the application of either party, a further appointment to fill any vacancy created by the nominee refusing to act, by his removal by the court, by incapacity or by his dying, where the parties do not themselves fill the vacancy within one month.

Reference is made in the clause to the Institution of Civil Engineers' Arbitration Procedure (1973): a document that was in fact published by the Institution in 1975. The President, when making an appointment, is empowered to direct that the reference shall be conducted in accordance with that procedure: but if he does not do so then the parties are free to choose whether or not to adopt it.

The above provisions of Clause 66 of the ICE Conditions constitute a good arbitration agreement in that it makes provision for the arbitrator to be appointed by a person who is able to choose one having appropriate technical knowledge, and if necessary for a replacement to be appointed by the same authority, where a vacancy arises. Unfortunately the clause also

ARBITRATION AGREEMENTS

makes other provisions in its 700 words: principally the requirement that any dispute or difference between the parties shall, as a preliminary to arbitration, be referred to the engineer for his decision. A period of three months is allowed for that decision: on receipt of the decision, or after the three months have elapsed, either party may within a period of a further three months give notice of arbitration.

The principal objection to this requirement is that it adds a further three months or more to the overall time required to settle a dispute; for the likelihood that the engineer's formal decision will be any more acceptable to an aggrieved party than his earlier decisions is remote indeed. Furthermore if it is thought by those responsible for drafting the clause that the need to make a formal decision will give warning to the engineer that his actions may lead to arbitration, then removal of that requirement should concentrate the engineer's mind on the seriousness of the position at an earlier stage in the negotiations. For, as in any other dispute, the parties rarely take action in either litigation or in arbitration without having tried to negotiate a settlement.

A further objection to what has become known as the 'two-stage' procedure under the ICE Conditions is that it may lead to attempts by an unscrupulous party to argue that a decision given more than three months earlier by the engineer constituted his decision under Clause 66, and that as the aggrieved party did not within the prescribed period give notice of arbitration he is now deemed to have accepted the engineer's decision. However the courts have ruled, in *Monmouth CC* v. *Costelloe & Kemple Ltd (1964)* that the engineer must make it quite clear that a statement is intended to be a decision under the clause.

Clause 66 of the ICE Conditions also seeks in general to preclude the commencement of arbitration proceedings until after completion, or alleged completion, of the works. Clearly the laudable aim of this requirement is to avoid the likely disruption to progress of the work where those involved in construction might find their time and energy diverted to the less productive activities involved in the reference. However an absolute prohibition of such proceedings during the course of construction could prevent a contractor from obtaining the payments needed to continue in business, thereby making it impossible for him to complete the works. Accordingly the somewhat draconian requirements of earlier editions of the conditions have been softened by providing for immediate arbitration of any dispute arising from Clause 12 of the conditions (which clause relates to payments in respect of adverse physical conditions and artificial obstructions) or from the withholding by the engineer of any certificate.

It was held in *A E Farr* v. *Ministry of Transport (1960)* that failure by the engineer to certify more than £15,000 of a proper claim by the contractor of £20,000 constituted 'withholding a certificate', in that case because of an error of law by the engineer; and accordingly the contractor was entitled to immediate arbitration. Whether the same rule would have applied to a reduction in the value of the certificate resulting from measurement differences is not clear. If the rule does so apply then effectively the contractor has a right to immediate arbitration of any substantial difference arising from the contract, but that right would not extend to cover a difference arising from an allegation of breach of contract.

The FCEC Form of Subcontract

The Form of Subcontract published by the Federation of Civil Engineering Contractors, which is designed for use in conjunction with the ICE Conditions of Contract, includes as Clause 18(1) a simple but adequate arbitration agreement. This provides for the arbitrator to be appointed by agreement between the parties, or failing agreement by the President of the ICE.

A situation that often arises in work performed by a subcontractor is that the real dispute is between the employer and the subcontractor: the main contractor, although a party to both main and subcontracts, is concerned only that his obligation under one of the contracts is reflected in a corresponding right under the other. If the subcontractor claims additional payment the main contractor will be willing to make that payment provided that he can recover the cost from the employer; and similarly if the employer rejects any parts of the works then the main contractor will be concerned to see that the rejection may be passed on as an obligation upon the subcontractor to make good the defects.

Clause 18(2) of the FCEC Form deals with this situation as far as it is possible to do so, by requiring the subcontractor to accept the arbitrator appointed under the main contract to act also under the subcontract. Hence where the dispute originates as a claim by the employer (for example an allegation of defective work) it is usually possible for the main contractor to use this subclause to ensure that the two references are consolidated under the same arbitrator.

Where the dispute originates as a claim by the subcontractor consolidation of a corresponding dispute between main contractor and employer can only be effected by agreement. It would however be possible for the main contractor to initiate an arbitration against the employer in respect of his subcontractor's claim, and then to require the subcontractor to accept the same arbitrator, under Clause 18(2).

Clause 18(3) of the FCEC Form covers the less likely possibility of the main contractor being involved in court proceedings in respect of a dispute that concerns the subcontract works. In such a situation the main contractor would wish to serve a third-party notice upon the subcontractor, but could be prevented from proceeding in such a manner by the subcontractor's applying for a stay of the court proceedings under Section 4 of the 1950 Act, on the ground that there is a valid arbitration agreement between the parties, to which the dispute should be referred. Clause 18(3) empowers the main contractor in this situation to abrogate the arbitration agreement.

The FIDIC Conditions of Contract

Under the Conditions of Contract (International) for Works of Civil Engineering Construction, better known as the FIDIC Conditions, the two-stage procedure of the ICE Conditions applies, with minor modifications to the wording. The arbitration agreement includes a provision that the Rules of Conciliation and Arbitration of the International Chamber of Commerce (ICC) shall apply.

The Standard Form of Building Contract

The Standard Form of Building Contract, published by the Joint Contracts Tribunal and often referred to as the JCT form, or incorrectly as the RIBA form, includes an arbitration agreement as Article 5 of the Form of Agreement. This provides for appointment of the arbitrator by agreement, or failing agreement within 14 days of one party serving upon the other a written notice to concur in the appointment of an arbitrator, for the arbitrator to be appointed by the President or a Vice-President of the RIBA.

The 1980 editions of the JCT Form introduce a new requirement corresponding to that of the FCEC Form, which seeks to ensure that where a dispute between the employer and the contractor is concerned with issues that are substantially the same as those between the contractor and a nominated subcontractor, both references to arbitration are dealt with by the same arbitrator. The Form does however recognise that this sensible provision is not always practicable, because the qualifications required of the arbitrator may not be the same in both cases.

3. Powers of an Arbitrator

Synopsis
An arbitrator derives his powers from the arbitration agreement between the parties (see Chapter 2) and from the 1950 and 1979 Acts. Provided that the agreement is valid and that he has been properly appointed the two Acts give him the basic powers needed to conduct the proceedings and to make an enforceable award. His powers may be extended by agreement between the parties, and where he considers it necessary for the proper conduct of the reference the arbitrator may seek such extension of his powers from the parties, or from the High Court.

Irrevocability of authority
Section 1 of the 1950 Act provides that the arbitrator's authority is irrevocable except by leave of the High Court or a judge thereof. Although the parties are in general able to adopt by agreement rules to expedite procedures, and are able to agree as to the appointment of the arbitrator, the Act sensibly excludes from these rights the right to remove an arbitrator once he has been appointed, except by leave of the High Court; and that court would, implicitly, have to be satisfied that there were adequate grounds for his removal.

It is however open to the appointed arbitrator to refuse to act: should he do so Section 10(b) of the 1950 Act provides a procedure for his replacement.

Conduct of proceedings
The principal power required by the arbitrator, namely that to order the parties to appear before him and to produce all relevant documents, is

POWERS OF AN ARBITRATOR

conferred under Section 12 of the 1950 Act by way of a deemed term in arbitration agreements that the parties shall do these things, and 'all other things which during the proceedings on the reference the arbitrator or umpire may require'. Certain other powers that may be needed, such as the power to subpoena a witness to appear and to give evidence at the hearing, are available to the parties but only upon application to the High Court.

Section 12(3) of the 1950 Act empowers the arbitrator to administer oaths or to take affirmations. Usually the arbitrator will require witnesses to swear or affirm, and he should always do so where credibility is in question.

Powers relating to the award

Other important powers conferred by the 1950 Act are:

Under Section 13: Power to make an award at any time: subject to the power of the High Court, on the application of either party, to remove an arbitrator who has failed to use reasonable dispatch in the proceedings.
Under Section 14: Power to make an interim award (see Chapter 8).
Under Section 15: Power to order specific performance (see Chapter 8).
Under Section 18: Power to award costs (see Chapter 9).
Under Section 20: Power to award interest (see Chapter 8).

Power to deal with a reluctant party

It sometimes happens before an arbitration is begun, or during its preliminary stages, that a party becomes aware of the weakness of its case and seeks to delay the proceedings as long as possible, in order to defer the day of settlement. The strategy usually adopted in such cases is to ignore the arbitrator's orders or to apply for excessive periods of time for preparation of pleadings; to apply for extensions; to apply for 'further and better particulars' (see Chapter 5) in unnecessary detail, or to fail to appear at meetings or at the hearing. Upon becoming aware of such action or inaction the arbitrator should proceed with the greatest of care in order to avoid undue prolongation of the reference, while ensuring that his award when published cannot be upset by the reluctant party.

He may in appropriate cases remind the parties of his power in relation to costs, making it clear that in the exercise of that power he will take into consideration either party's responsibility for any costs that may have been incurred unnecessarily in abortive meetings or in dealing with unwarranted applications for extension of time.

Usually an arbitrator will grant a reasonable first application for an extension of time for delivery of pleadings, where he is satisfied that it arises from some valid cause such as sickness of the person who has to prepare the pleading. Should there be a second application the arbitrator will probably invite the other party to comment upon it before coming to a decision, and in a case where the application is opposed, will hear the application and the objection to it at a meeting called for that purpose. The costs of such a meeting will be awarded against the defaulting party or against the party making the application unless there is some good reason to the contrary.

Where a party fails to deliver pleadings by the due date, and fails to apply for an extension of time, the arbitrator may, if he thinks fit, call a meeting of both parties in order to hear the defaulting party's reasons for the failure, and any application that the opposing party may make for an order either to deliver the pleading by a certain date, or to provide details—usually of the defence—at that meeting or at a meeting called for the purpose.

If the party in default fails to attend this meeting or any other meeting the arbitrator should firstly allow a reasonable period of time— perhaps an hour depending upon circumstances—to cover the possibility that the party may be delayed in his journey. During the period of waiting he must be careful to avoid discussing the arbitration with the other party: he will usually withdraw to remove any suspicion that this may have happened. When it becomes clear that there is nothing to be gained by further waiting the arbitrator should adjourn the meeting. He should then write to both parties, fixing another date for the meeting, warning the parties that if either fails to appear he will proceed *ex parte* (that is, in the absence of that party) and marking his order 'PEREMPTORY'. Having taken these precautions, and having of course satisfied himself that the party in default has received the order, the arbitrator may hear an application from the party present and make an appropriate order.

Where it becomes necessary a similar procedure may be adopted by the arbitrator in conducting an *ex parte* hearing: and in such a case he should ensure that the claimant's case is proved before making an award in his favour.

Until the 1979 Act became law a problem could arise where a reluctant respondent ignored the arbitrator's orders as to interlocutory matters such as pleadings and discovery, but arrived at the hearing in order to present a defence. The arbitrator had no power to refuse permission to the respondent to take part: but to allow the hearing to proceed would put the claimant at a disadvantage because he had not been forewarned of the respondent's defence. So he would have to grant a further adjournment, having ascertained the nature of the defence, in order that the claimant could deal with the points raised in that defence.

Section 5 of the 1979 Act greatly strengthens the arbitrator's power to deal with such tactics, by permitting him, or the other party, to apply to the High Court for an order extending the arbitrator's powers in a case where a party fails within the time specified, or within a reasonable time, to comply with his orders. An order granted under this section could, subject to any limitation that may be imposed by the court, empower the arbitrator to continue with the reference in the way that a High Court judge might deal with a similar situation in that court: that is, by making an order debarring the respondent from defending the claim at all, leaving it to the claimant to prove his case unhindered by the respondent. Such an order could where appropriate be applied to that part of the claim which is affected by the respondent's failure to comply with the arbitrator's order.

Similarly, where the claimant fails to proceed with reasonable dispatch the arbitrator or the respondent may now apply to the court for an order enabling the arbitrator to strike out all or the relevant parts of a claim.

4. Appointment of the Arbitrator

Synopsis
A party wishing to refer a dispute to arbitration should comply strictly with the terms of the arbitration agreement in giving notice of arbitration and in initiating the appointment of the arbitrator. The person appointed must be properly qualified to act. Provision is made in the two main statutes for filling a vacancy that arises through the breakdown of machinery for appointment or through the appointed person ceasing to be available.

Procedure for appointment
The first rule in initiating proceedings is to comply strictly with the arbitration agreement. Thus for instance if the contract incorporates the ICE Conditions of Contract or some derivative of that document such as FIDIC it is necessary to give notice to the engineer that a dispute has arisen, specifying the cause of the dispute, and requiring his decision under Clause 66 of the contract. If he replies within three months giving an unsatisfactory decision or if he fails to reply within three months then in either case the arbitration proper may be commenced.

The ICE and many other forms of contract provide for the appointment of an arbitrator *failing agreement* by the named authority: the President of the ICE in the case of a contract under that Institution's contract. Hence an attempt should be made to agree upon an arbitrator, the usual form of such an attempt being a letter from the applicant putting forward the names of up to three engineers, any one of whom would be acceptable to the applicant (see SD/6). Where the ICE Conditions apply the Notice of Arbitration and Notice to Concur may be given on Form ArbICE published by the Institution (see SD/3 and 4).

If the other party—usually the respondent—disagrees with all of the suggestions, or if he fails to reply within a reasonable period (one calendar month under the ICE form) then application may be made to the President of the ICE (see SD/5) or in the case of other forms of agreement to the appointing authority named in the agreement. The ICE and many other authorities charge a fee for the administrative work associated with the appointment: in the case of the ICE the current fee is £40 plus VAT.

Qualifications of the arbitrator

The first and most important qualification of any arbitrator is that he must not have any interest in or relationship with either party such as might impair his impartiality. He must not be a friend or relative of either party; nor must he have any prior knowledge of the subject matter of the dispute, as distinct from a general knowledge of the type of work involved in the dispute, which is necessary. He must not have a financial interest in either party, for example as a shareholder or as a consultant. A prior relationship that no longer exists or a distant relationship by blood or by marriage need not be a bar provided that the arbitrator knows that it will not affect his judgment; but in such a case he should disclose the relationship to both parties and be willing to stand down if either party objects to his appointment.

It sometimes happens that the existence of a link with one of the parties becomes known to the arbitrator only after he has accepted the appointment. In such a case he should, if the relationship is such as to affect his impartiality, withdraw as soon as the facts become known to him. In other cases, where his impartiality is not affected, he should nevertheless disclose the relationship to both parties and be prepared to withdraw if required to do so by either party. He is not debarred from withdrawing by Section 1 of the 1950 Act because his action would be to refuse to act: and the parties are free under Section 10(b) of that Act to agree upon a replacement or failing agreement to apply to the court for an appointment.

Secondly the arbitrator should have a general knowledge of the technicalities of the matters in dispute. The extent of this knowledge must depend to a large extent upon the technicality and variety of the issues that arise. It would not for example be reasonable to expect the arbitrator to have a specialised knowledge of a wide variety of engineering subjects; in such cases the arbitrator's general knowledge of the variety of subjects might have to be supplemented by expert evidence brought by the parties. On the other hand it is to be expected that a dispute involving road and bridge works would be referred to an arbitrator having that type of experience: not for example to a specialist in water supply.

If the arbitrator finds, either before or after his appointment, that the dispute concerns a matter of which he has prior knowledge—for example, one in which he has given specialist advice, or has made a study for some other purpose, then he should decline or withdraw from the appointment, as the case may be. This is because of the danger that that prior knowledge may influence his decision: his duty in the arbitration is to decide the issues upon the evidence presented.

Thirdly the arbitrator should have judicial capacity. He should be able to consider and weigh the evidence presented by the parties; to reach a logical decision based upon that evidence upon matters of fact; and to make a just award. He is the judge both of fact and of law and should therefore have a basic knowledge of the law of contract and of tort, together with a sufficient knowledge of the law of evidence to enable him to give just rulings upon the admissibility of the evidence presented.

Terms of the appointment

Whether chosen by agreement or appointed by an authority it is the arbitrator himself who chooses whether or not to accept the appointment. He may possibly require as a condition of his appointment that the parties agree to his scale of charges, but usually it is unwise for him to insist that both parties must agree. This is because refusal to agree may simply be a ploy in a reluctant party's strategy of delay.

Where the arbitrator has been chosen by agreement between the parties it is usual for the claimant to notify him of that agreement and to request that he accepts the appointment and proceeds with the reference. Where appointed by the President of the ICE or some other authority the arbitrator and the parties will be notified by the authority of the appointment.

Opinions differ among arbitrators as to whether or not they should state the basis of their charges and other conditions of appointment at the outset of the reference. The ICE booklet *Arbitration Procedure (1973)* provides for their doing so, and certainly all arbitrators should state the basis of their charges—usually as a rate per hour or per day plus their expenses plus VAT—if requested by either party to do so. On the other hand the 1950 Act makes sensible provision for dealing with the point where no agreement has been made, in that Section 18(1) empowers the arbitrator to 'tax and settle' the amount of his charges (which are referred to as the 'costs of the award'), while Section 19 empowers a party, after paying the costs demanded into court, to have those costs taxed in the High Court. Where a scale has been

APPOINTMENT OF THE ARBITRATOR

quoted by the arbitrator and that scale has been agreed by both parties then it is of course binding upon them and upon the arbitrator. Where neither party has agreed, or only one has agreed, the arbitrator should, if he intends to proceed, notify the parties that he will in due course tax and settle his fees under Section 18 of the 1950 Act (see Chapter 9).

Arbitrators usually require as a condition of their appointment that they are empowered to take legal advice; the cost of such advice is part of the costs of the award.

Supplying vacancies

It sometimes happens that after being appointed the arbitrator refuses to act (for example because he has become aware of some bar to his acting or for some other reason) or becomes incapable of acting, or dies. These situations are dealt with in Clause 66 of the ICE Conditions and more generally under Section 10 of the 1950 Act, by which a party may serve on the other a notice to concur in the appointment of a replacement. If the other party fails to concur within seven days, the party who gave the notice may apply to the High Court to make an appointment.

A further difficulty that may arise, and one which was not foreseen in the 1950 Act, is that an appointing authority named in an arbitration agreement may neglect or refuse or be unable to make an appointment. This gap in the 1950 Act has been dealt with by way of an amendment to Section 10, enacted as part of Section 6 of the 1979 Act, which covers such failures and provides for appointment by notice to concur or by the High Court, as in other cases.

5. Preliminaries

Synopsis
Before matters in dispute can be brought to a hearing the issues to be determined must be defined. Each party must be forewarned of the case it has to answer: relevant documents must be disclosed and where possible agreed. Arrangements as to representation and appointment of experts must be defined and notified: and arrangements for the hearing must be made.

English law
It is a basic principle of English law that surprise tactics shall not be used, either in litigation or in arbitration. Neither party is allowed to gain an advantage by, for example, appointing leading or junior counsel to represent them at the hearing without giving notice of that intention, or by making some allegation that has not been disclosed to the other party and for which that other party has been unable to prepare. Neither party may without notice call an expert to give evidence, because without such notice the other party would be unable to appoint its expert—possibly to express a different opinion.

English law also requires that all documents relevant to the matters in dispute must be disclosed to the other party, whether or not they support the case of the party holding them. These two requirements of the law are dealt with during the preliminary or 'interlocutory' stages of an arbitration, and are termed 'pleadings' and 'discovery of documents'. But there are also other matters, such as special rules of procedure, and the time-table for the various stages, which may need to be defined: preferably at the beginning of the proceedings.

The preliminary meeting

Sometimes called a 'meeting for directions', the preliminary meeting is a meeting between both parties' representatives and the arbitrator, usually called by the arbitrator as soon as he has accepted his appointment, in order that procedures, arrangements and a time-table may be agreed and defined. Such definition is given in an 'Order for Directions' issued to both parties by the arbitrator after the meeting (see SD/12).

Alternatively an Order for Directions may sometimes be agreed in correspondence between the parties and sent as a draft to the arbitrator, who will then issue a formal Order by consent. Disadvantages of this procedure are that it provides no opportunity for the arbitrator to ascertain the nature and magnitude of the matters in dispute, of which he may at this stage have little if any knowledge; it provides no opportunity for the arbitrator to influence the parties into agreeing upon simplifying procedures and agreeing upon as short periods of time for the various stages as may be practicable, or for any discussion between the parties and the arbitrator; and the draft Order as prepared by the parties may not cover all of the matters that need to be defined. On the other hand it saves the time and cost of a meeting, and this may be an important consideration where the parties and the arbitrator are in widely scattered locations.

A check list of matters that may need to be discussed at the preliminary meeting is given in SD/11. In addition there may be other matters to be considered: where, for example, the terms of the arbitrator's appointment need further definition, or where his authority is in question or is subject to some restriction, or where liability is to be dealt with separately from quantum.

If he has not already done so the arbitrator should ensure at the preliminary meeting that his appointment is in order. He should check the contract and the arbitration clause therein; that the procedure for his appointment has been followed properly; that the subject matter of the dispute is within his own expertise but that he has no prior knowledge of the particular dispute with which he is to be concerned; and finally that he has no relationship or interest which might, or might be thought to, impair his impartiality. He may, if he has not already done so, agree the terms of his appointment with the parties, and confirm those terms in letters to both parties after the meeting.

The next step at the preliminary meeting is to define the parties' intentions as to representation and as to the appointment of experts, as these matters will affect the time needed for preparation of the pleadings, and the later stages of the arbitration.

Where both parties elect to appoint counsel the arbitrator will usually deem the proceedings to be 'fit for counsel' and will mark his Orders and Directions in the proceedings accordingly. By so doing he will enable each party to include counsel's fees and expenses in its bill of costs at the conclusion of the reference. Where both parties agree not to appoint counsel there is no difficulty. But where one party insists upon appointing against the wishes of the other, it will be for the arbitrator to decide, probably later in the proceedings, as to whether or not the appointment was necessary, and to mark papers accordingly. In some cases the party not wishing to appoint counsel may feel itself obliged by the action of the other party to do so; in such a case the arbitrator should consider whether or not to require the party who insists upon counsel to bear both parties' counsels' costs in any event—that is, irrespective of the outcome of the claim.

Pleadings

Pleadings have been defined as statements in writing served by each party alternately upon the other stating the facts relied upon to support its case and giving such details as the opposing party may need to know in order to prepare its case. Besides providing a means of forewarning each party of the case of its opponent, pleadings serve as a means of defining the questions of fact and of law that have to be determined by the arbitrator. Each document in the pleadings must state material facts only, in summary form, and not the evidence by which those facts are to be proved.

Documents in the pleadings comprise Points of Claim, Points of Defence, and Points of Reply (see SD/13, 14 and 15). The reply provides an opportunity for the claimant to deal with any allegations in the Points of Defence that are not mere rebuttals of the Points of Claim; the Points of Reply must not raise any new allegations.

Where there is a counterclaim—that is, a claim by the respondent against the claimant—it is pleaded with the Points of Defence, the words 'and Counterclaim' being added to the title, and details being given at the end of the defence. Thereafter the pleadings relating to the counterclaim follow one step behind those relating to the claim: the Defence to Counterclaim being pleaded with the Points of Reply, and where necessary there may also be a Reply to Defence to Counterclaim.

In order to facilitate reference to their content each of the pleadings should contain a series of numbered paragraphs each of which deals with a single subject. Points of Claim should commence with a brief introduction of the parties and should then identify the contract from which the dispute arises: its purpose and an outline of the respective responsibilities and rights of the parties. Next it is usual to identify and summarise the particular clauses of the contract that are relevant to the matters in dispute, and to state in what way those clauses—or where appropriate, terms that may be implied into the contract—have been breached. Finally the Points of Claim should state what damage was suffered by the claimant as a result of the breaches of the contract.

Damages may in this context be defined as the loss suffered as a result of the breach of contract; the legal principle governing their assessment is that the injured party should be put as nearly as possible in the same position as he would have been had there been no breach. There are two main categories: special damages, which are not presumed at law, but must be expressly pleaded and proved; and general damages, which follow naturally from the wrong pleaded, and need not therefore be pleaded.

Where the arbitration arises from rejection of a claim for additional payment, the damages claimed are likely to be wholly special damages, which must be pleaded and particularised in full. In such cases the breach complained of should be defined, and the special damages claimed should be set out in a schedule of particulars: where necessary there should be such a schedule for each breach pleaded.

The basic rule in drafting Points of Defence is that any allegation in the Points of Claim that is not denied or otherwise dealt with is deemed to be admitted. There are three ways in which the respondent may deal with an allegation in the Points of Claim: he may admit, deny, or 'not admit' it.

In most cases there are several statements in the claim that are not in dispute: for example the existence of the contract, its purpose, and the content of clauses in it. In such cases the Points of Defence should admit those statements: but it may at the same time be desirable to draw attention to other documents, or clauses in the contract, which have not been quoted in the Points of Claim because they do not favour the claimant's case.

Secondly there may be allegations in the Points of Claim which the respondent believes to be untrue, and these must be denied. Thirdly there may be allegations relating to matters of which the respondent has insufficient knowledge either to admit or to deny. Where such allegations are important to the claimant's case the respondent may state in the defence that they are 'not admitted'—thereby requiring the claimant to prove them.

Besides dealing with each of the allegations in the Points of Claim the Points of Defence may include fresh allegations; for example, in a case in which the claimant alleges that his work was delayed through some fault of the employer or of his engineer, an allegation that the delay was caused by some inadequacy in the contractor's organisation. Finally, it is usual in most cases to include a 'blanket denial' of all allegations not specifically admitted (see paragraph 3 of SD/14) to cover the possibility that some of the items in the Points of Claim may not have been dealt with adequately.

In some cases a party may consider that the pleadings are not sufficiently detailed to give that party proper forewarning of the case to be answered. In such a situation the party should serve a Request for Further and Better Particulars (see SD/16).

Amendment of pleadings
During the course of the pleadings, during later stages of the interlocutories, or even during the hearing, a need may arise to amend pleadings, for example when the Points of Defence disclose some fact not previously known to the claimant, or where fresh evidence comes to light during discovery or during the hearing. In such cases the party wishing to amend its pleadings should apply to the arbitrator for his consent, giving reasons for the application, and of course sending a copy to the other party. Generally, such a request, if soundly based, will be granted, with the proviso that the applicant shall bear any costs that may result from the amendment, in any event; that is, irrespective of the outcome of the arbitration.

There are however exceptions to this general rule. Where for example the need to make the amendment arises from some fault on the part of the other party, the party making the application should bring the fault to the notice of the arbitrator, and request that he exercise his discretion as to costs (see Chapter 9). If there is a dispute between the parties as to who should bear the costs of the amendment, the arbitrator may possibly reserve his decision on the point, or may call a meeting at which he will hear both parties' contentions before coming to a decision.

The amount of costs that may result from an amendment of the pleadings may vary widely according to the extent of the amendment and the stage at which it is allowed. In most cases, where the application to amend is made during the pleadings or during discovery, the amendment will result in a need for subsequent pleadings also to be amended; the costs of such amendments will fall upon the applicant for the original amendment, subject to the exceptions referred to above. An application to amend made during discovery is likely, in addition, to involve delay; while an application to amend pleadings made during the hearing will, if granted, usually require adjournment of the hearing and will therefore involve the costs of time allocated to it by the parties and their representatives and witnesses and by the arbitrator. Such a situation may arise where a party alleges, during the hearing, that evidence being presented by his opponent relates to matters that were not disclosed in the pleadings. If the arbitrator upholds the allegation, then he may ask the party giving evidence if he wishes to apply to amend his pleadings; otherwise he must require the party to abandon the evidence in question. In considering which course to adopt the amount of costs likely to be incurred if the amendment proceeds, may be an important factor affecting the applicant's decision.

The Scott Schedule
Where a claim comprises a large number of items each of which has a separate basis in the contract, it is often convenient for the arbitrator to have the pleadings summarised in the form of a Scott Schedule, sometimes called an Official Referee's Schedule. Such a schedule usually requires preparation by both parties, and does not have any fixed format, other than the basic principle that each item is taken separately, and includes the contentions of both parties in relation to that item (see SD/18).

Discovery of documents
After the close of pleadings, each party must prepare lists of documents (see SD/19) that are or have been in the party's 'possession or power' relating to the matters in dispute, and must serve a copy of the lists upon the opposing party. All documents listed, other than those that are 'privileged', must be made available for inspection by the other party, and if required, copies must be made at the expense of the party requiring the copies. On completion of discovery and inspection the parties should compile an agreed list of documents, being an amalgam of both parties' lists, and should ensure that each document is serially numbered. Copies of documents should then be prepared for the use of each party and of the arbitrator at the hearing: so that each document may be readily identified and referred to while evidence is being given.

The requirement to disclose all relevant documents is observed strictly, and applies not only to those documents that support the case of the party holding them, but also to documents that detract from that case. The principle is that the arbitrator requires to discover the truth; any document that helps to throw light on that truth, however embarrassing it may be, is of value to the arbitrator. Thus for example a contractor who is seeking enhanced payment in respect of an item of varied work must expect to have to disclose pricing notes showing the make-up of the original rate. Again, correspondence between the employer and the main contractor may well be relevant to a dispute between main and subcontractor, especially where inadequacy in the subcontractor's work is alleged.

Usually the relevant documents in a dispute arising from a construction contract comprise all of the contract documents and drawings, all correspondence between the parties and between the contractor and the engineer, including drawings, instructions, variation orders and certificates issued during the course of the works; site diaries; interim valuations submitted by the contractor during the course of the works; the final account; the contractor's office records of wages, plant, oncosts, daywork sheets, pricing notes, internal memos and correspondence between the site agent and his head office. Additionally there may also be relevant correspondence between the contractor and third parties such as subcontractors, suppliers and technical advisers.

Where a party suspects that not all relevant documents have been discovered by its opponent the party may serve a notice requiring an affidavit verifying the list of documents, or requiring a statement as to what has become of a document known to have existed.

Usually a dispute between the parties arising from an allegation of incomplete discovery is resolved between them, but if necessary a party may apply to the arbitrator for an order requiring the opposing party to discover the documents in question. Failure to comply with such an order would provide grounds for the aggrieved party to apply to the High Court under Section 12(6) of the 1950 Act for an order requiring discovery.

Privilege

Certain types of document need not be produced on discovery, although they must be included in the list of documents, in a separate schedule marked to indicate that privilege is claimed. Privilege relates to correspondence between clients and their legal advisers; more generally to any letter or document prepared with a view to litigation or arbitration, and to offers to settle the dispute, where marked 'without prejudice'. It is sometimes claimed that certain documents should be privileged because they contain confidential information. Such claims can rarely be upheld, because arbitration proceedings are private, and confidentiality, which might otherwise be a factor, is of minor importance. In *Mitchell Construction Kinnear Moodie Group* v. *East Anglia Regional Hospital Board (1971)* personal files relating to the contractor's employees were ordered to be disclosed, it being held that the sole issue was one of relevance. Similar principles would be applied to the discovery of other private documents, internal memoranda, pricing and estimating notes, where they can be shown to be relevant to the matters in issue.

Agreement of figures and documents
The Order for Directions usually includes an order that 'figures shall be agreed as figures' and that documents, plans, photographs, etc. shall be agreed where possible.

The purpose of the order relating to figures is to obviate the need to bring detailed evidence during the hearing, on such matters as the total cost of items of work, or on records of numbers of men engaged during the course of the works. A contractor's detailed records of such matters is not usually a point of contention: by agreeing upon the summary of total cost of labour, plant and materials, expensive time at the hearing may be saved.

Documents produced in evidence should where possible have been agreed so that they may be included in agreed bundles, available for reference during the hearing. Documents that have not been agreed must be 'proved' by calling as a witness the person who prepared or issued the document, who will state that he did so.

Transcript of the hearing
If the arbitrator thinks it necessary he may seek the parties' agreement to there being made a transcript of the hearing, or of part of it (for example, the closing addresses by both counsel), but he may not order such a transcript without the consent of both parties. The cost of attendance of a shorthand writer, and of transcribing, may be a major item in the total costs of the reference, and for this reason many arbitrators are content to rely upon their own notes, possibly supplemented by a tape recording of proceedings at the hearing. In such cases the arbitrator will himself make the recording, taking a careful note of tape numbers and recorder meter readings at important events, such as the start of each witness's evidence. This will enable him to refer without undue difficulty to any passage in the evidence, so that he can ascertain the actual words used by the witness where contention arises.

Arrangements for the hearing
Unless the arbitration agreement determines otherwise, the arbitrator has absolute discretion as to the date, time and place of the hearing. He should however exercise that discretion reasonably, bearing in mind that one of the reasons for the choice of arbitration is that it seeks to serve the convenience of the parties.

Where a large number of witnesses are required, and especially where solicitors and counsel are appointed, choosing a date or dates suitable to everyone concerned may present difficulty. For this reason it is usually desirable to fix at least a provisional date for the start of the hearing either at the preliminary meeting or soon afterwards, so that dates may be reserved by everyone concerned. By raising this point at the preliminary meeting the arbitrator can hear the parties' wishes and can comply with them as far as is reasonable and possible.

The location of the hearing may have been determined in the arbitration agreement; but whether or not this is so the parties are free to agree upon a location best suited to the convenience of all of those concerned. In major cases this often means London, because many counsel and major firms of solicitors are based there; other locations may be considered upon their merits. The arbitrator will be wise to ensure that the chosen location is one in which the procedural law of the arbitration applies: meaning, for example, a location in either England or Wales if the arbitration is to be conducted in accordance with English law.

The venue of the hearing should be a court room, hall or office sufficiently large to accommodate all of those involved in reasonable comfort, and having regard to the probable need to refer to and perhaps to display large numbers of documents and drawings. The usual layout of the court room provides two long and parallel tables, one for each party, and a linking table across one end at which the arbitrator sits. Witnesses, when called, sit facing the arbitrator between the two parallel tables, so that their evidence and demeanour may be heard and seen by both parties and by the arbitrator. In smaller or less formal hearings the parties may sit on either side of a single large table, with the arbitrator at the head, and with witnesses when called either at the foot of the table or in whatever position enables them to be best heard and seen.

Accommodation for the hearing is sometimes booked by the arbitrator and sometimes by one of the parties: probably the claimant. In some cases a party may offer the use of its premises for the hearing: such an offer should not be accepted by the arbitrator without the agreement of the other party.

Conduct of interlocutory stages

The arbitrator should at all times exercise the greatest care in ensuring that he is, and that he is seen to be, impartial in his dealings with both parties. He should not have any communication with a party without the knowledge of the other; this in practice means that he either writes letters addressed to both parties, or when writing to one party sends a copy to the other. He should ensure that a copy of any letter he receives from one party is sent to the other, either by the writer or by himself, and he should avoid having any communication by telephone, except possibly for the purpose of arranging dates for meetings, in which case the outcome of those conversations should be notified to both parties.

For similar reasons he should avoid having any meeting with a party except in the presence of the other: and he should not accept hospitality from either party, even in the presence of the other.

'Liberty to apply'

Most Orders for Directions contain an order that there shall be liberty to apply. This phrase originates from practice in the courts, in which it means that the parties may come to the court again without taking out a fresh summons. Hence, in arbitration it may not be strictly necessary, but it serves to indicate that a party may where necessary apply to the arbitrator for an extension of time, for permission to amend pleadings, for a meeting or hearing, or for an order requiring the other party to take any action that may be needed during the interlocutory stages.

Questions of law arising during a reference

It sometimes becomes clear during the interlocutory proceedings that the success of a claim, or of a substantial part of it, depends upon a question of law which, if determined as a preliminary matter, might save unnecessary delay and costs. Where for example it is pleaded that the circumstances of a claim bar it from consideration because of the operation of the Limitation Acts, such a defence, if successful, would obviate the need to proceed further.

The arbitrator has jurisdiction to determine questions of law, and he may do so either from his own knowledge or, where appropriate, he may take legal advice on the issues involved—provided that by so doing he does not delegate his authority to another person. Either of these courses will however leave the possibility that the question may be determined incorrectly.

Provision is made in the 1979 Act for such questions to be determined by the High Court, subject to compliance with certain requirements. Under Section 2 of the Act, an application to the court must be made by one of the parties, either with the consent of the arbitrator or with the consent of the other party (or parties, where there are more than two). The arbitrator is not himself empowered to make such an application, although in appropriate cases he could suggest this course of action to the parties and indicate that he would give his consent to an application by one of them if this consent should be needed.

In considering an application under this section the High Court requires to be satisfied that determination of the question of law might produce a substantial saving in costs, and secondly that it could substantially affect the rights of one or more of the parties.

Applications under this section are dealt with in the Commercial Court of the Queen's Bench Division, and it is to be expected that they will normally be dealt with as matters of urgency.

Small claims
It is reasonable in this context to define small claims as those in which a risk exists that costs may be substantial in relation to the sum in dispute. The objective of procedures designed to deal with such claims is to ensure that costs are not allowed to become disproportionate to the claims; hence the definition is itself flexible. However as a very rough guide it is suggested that any claim amounting to less than five figures is potentially within this definition.

In many such cases the parties will not have appointed legal or technical representatives at the time of commencing the arbitration, and they may have little knowledge of their rights and duties during the reference; still less of their rights to agree with the other party upon simplifying procedures. The arbitrator should therefore make it clear to both parties that they have the right to be represented—provided that the arbitration agreement does not specify otherwise—upon giving notice of this intention, or to conduct their own cases. He should also make it clear that the costs of such representation may be substantial, and that the question who should ultimately bear the costs lies within his discretion.

On the assumption that one or both parties may opt not to be represented, and that that party or parties may not be familiar with arbitration procedure, the arbitrator may think it desirable to outline such procedure: an example of a letter setting out the basic information is given on sheet SD/9.

Where the sum in dispute is so small as not even to warrant a hearing, and provided that justice can be done without, the arbitrator may suggest a 'documents only' reference, as set out in SD/10.

6. Evidence

Synopsis
Evidence may be defined as all legal means whereby matters of fact may be proved or disproved. The law of evidence is highly complex; while the rules deriving from the law need not be applied rigidly in arbitration, and may be varied by agreement between the parties, the principles upon which the rules are based should not be abandoned without good cause. In this chapter the kinds of evidence and rules relating to its presentation are outlined.

Statutes
The principal statutes governing the law of evidence are the Evidence Act 1938, the Civil Evidence Act 1968, and the Civil Evidence Act 1972. The 1968 Act relates mainly to rules governing the admissibility of hearsay evidence, while the 1972 Act deals with expert evidence.

Kinds of evidence
The main types of evidence adduced in construction arbitrations are documentary, oral and real evidence. There are however several other ways in which different kinds of evidence may be distinguished: for example it may be evidence of fact or of opinion; it may be direct or circumstantial; it may be primary or secondary. Hence any item of evidence may be categorised in several different ways, depending upon the manner in which it is adduced, and upon its content and quality.

DOCUMENTARY EVIDENCE
Under this heading is included all evidence in writing or on paper: letters,

documents, drawings, photographs, computer print-outs and the like. All documents that are relevant to the matters in issue must be discovered (see p. 27), including those for which privilege is claimed, and those which are not privileged must be made available for inspection and for copying.

In many construction arbitrations documentary evidence is by far the most important factor in determining the matters in question, especially where the parties have maintained comprehensive records and where a long interval elapses between events giving rise to the dispute and the arbitration.

In general the documents produced in evidence must be originals: the letter sent from one party to another, not the file copy retained by the sender. It should be noted however that the manner in which the document was originally prepared—whether as the original typed letter, as a carbon or photocopy or by any other means—is immaterial; the letter that was signed and sent is the original, even though it may have been prepared by photocopying.

Where the original document has been lost or destroyed a copy may be admissible.

It is a duty of the arbitrator to ensure that, where required under the Stamp Act 1891, documents taken in evidence must be adequately stamped, and he should not accept such evidence until any deficiency in stamping has been corrected.

ORAL EVIDENCE

The arbitrator is empowered, under Section 12(3) of the 1950 Act, to administer oaths or to take affirmations of the parties and of their witnesses, and usually that power is exercised. A witness who knowingly makes a false statement under oath is guilty of perjury, which is punishable by fine or by imprisonment, or both.

Where necessary a party to a reference may compel a witness to attend the hearing, by means of a writ of *subpoena ad testificandum*; and a Master of the High Court is empowered to issue such a writ to compel the attendance of any witness living in the United Kingdom.

Where evidence is required from a person who cannot readily be brought to the hearing a party may apply to bring evidence on affidavit, that is, a sworn statement; where necessary an order in respect of such evidence may be obtained from the High Court. Such evidence is however of less value than that given orally, because it provides no opportunity for cross-examination.

REAL EVIDENCE

Material objects presented for examination are termed real evidence. They may be samples brought to the hearing, such as bricks, pieces of concrete, steel sections and so forth, or they may be immovable objects such as bridges or dams, which have to be inspected on site. Where necessary the arbitrator may either before, during or after the hearing arrange to inspect real evidence on site, in the presence of both parties' representatives, who should be permitted to draw matters to his attention but not to make any representation to him.

EVIDENCE OF FACT

Unless a witness is qualified as an expert (see below) his evidence must be of factual matters only, and of matters that are within his personal knowledge. He is not permitted to express opinions.

In many cases however the facts upon which opinions are based are of more evidential value than the opinions themselves: for example a statement of the dates on which drawings were issued in relation to the programme for construction of the works shown on them is likely to carry more weight than an opinion that the drawings were issued late. Similarly a statement that a brick wall is 30mm out of plumb and contains courses varying from 72 to 77mm in height is of more value than a subjective opinion that the workmanship of the brickwork is of poor quality.

The Civil Evidence Act 1972 does however relax the rules relating to evidence of opinion, as outlined in the following paragraphs.

EXPERT EVIDENCE

A witness may be called to give evidence of opinion on matters in which he is suitably qualified. Such a witness is termed an expert and his appointment and evidence is subject to special rules, principally those contained in the Civil Evidence Act 1972. The role of an expert is to assist the arbitrator in coming to a correct decision on the points for which he is called to give evidence: he is not in any sense an advocate for the party calling him. For this reason an expert should not accept an appointment as such until he is sure that the evidence he is able to give will support the case of the party proposing to call him. Having satisfied himself on this point, and having accepted the appointment, he must still direct his evidence to elucidation of the truth rather than the mere presentation of his party's case. This does not imply that he should make the opposing party's case for him: but he should be aware of any weaknesses in his evidence and should give it with honesty and sincerity.

An expert's qualifications as such need not necessarily be formal, such as degrees of universities or membership of learned bodies. In some cases experience may be the prime requirement: for example where an issue arises from a claim under Clause 12 of the ICE Conditions as to whether or not conditions or obstructions encountered by the contractor were such as might reasonably have been foreseen by an experienced contractor, the appropriate expert would be an experienced contractor.

The rules as to who may give evidence of opinion have been relaxed under the Civil Evidence Act 1972, in that a person called as a witness of fact may give a statement of opinion on any matter on any relevant matter on which he is qualified. Moreover he may give a statement of opinion on other matters for which he is not qualified, where that statement conveys relevant facts perceived by him personally.

HEARSAY EVIDENCE

One of the rules of evidence is that statements made by another person to a witness are not admissible unless the other person is the opposing party or his agent, or unless the statement was made in the presence of the opposing party or his agent. In general, the maker of the original statement should be called to give the evidence; and even where the rules allow hearsay evidence to be admitted it is of less weight than that of the originator of the statement.

This basic rule has however been relaxed under the Civil Evidence Act 1968, which allows hearsay evidence to be admitted by leave of the court, subject to certain rules. These permit, for example, hearsay evidence of what a witness said on some previous occasion to be admitted after that witness has given his evidence-in-chief, thereby allowing inconsistencies in the witness's evidence to be brought to light.

Admissibility of evidence

The primary requirement of evidence in order that it may be admitted is that it must be relevant to the points at issue. It is for the arbitrator to decide any question as to admissibility, but generally, where the parties are legally represented, he need not reject any evidence unless an objection is raised by the other party. Where a party is not so represented however, he may think it necessary to draw attention to any defect in the evidence being presented by the other and to invite an objection.

The arbitrator should not refuse to hear any admissible evidence: but should it appear to him that a point has already been adequately covered and is being laboured unnecessarily, he may suggest to the party bringing the evidence that he has already heard enough evidence on that point.

Proofs of evidence

A witness of fact is not permitted to read from a prepared statement, or even to refer to such a statement, while giving evidence. He is however permitted to refer to notes taken contemporaneously with the events referred to—for example his diary.

In order to assist the solicitor or counsel conducting his examination-in-chief it is usual for the evidence of each witness to be called to be set down as a proof of evidence, to which counsel will refer while examining the witness. By skilful questioning he will bring out all of the points that need to be covered by the witness.

An expert witness is however permitted to refer to his report or other statement prepared by him after the event, while giving his evidence. Nevertheless it is usual for counsel to prepare a proof of expert evidence in a similar way to that of a witness of fact, so that counsel may ensure that important points are covered and emphasised as necessary.

An example of a proof of evidence is given in SD/20.

Calling witnesses

The arbitrator is not empowered to call witnesses; only the parties may do so. Should it appear to the arbitrator that some person ought to be able to give evidence on the matters in issue, or that some point may not be covered, he can bring the omission to the notice of the parties by an enquiry whether, for example, the engineer under the contract is to be called, or whether he will be hearing evidence on the point that needs to be covered. If he finds that the point needs to be dealt with by a person who has already given evidence he can ask the party in question to recall that witness for further questioning.

Burden and standard of proof

The burden of proving an assertion made by a party lies with that party. Having provided such proof, the burden shifts to the other party who will have either to disprove the assertion, or show that it is not a material point in dealing with the main issues, in order to return the burden again to the party making the assertion.

In arbitration, as in civil actions in court, the standard of proof required is that of *preponderance of probability*. If it appears to the arbitrator more probable than not that events were as stated by a party he will find in favour of that party. This standard may be contrasted with that required in the criminal courts, in which the prosecution must prove guilt *beyond reasonable doubt* in order to obtain a conviction.

7. The Hearing

Synopsis
Rules governing attendance at the hearing; privacy; courtesy; challenges to jurisdiction; procedure and sequence.

Attendance
Notwithstanding that the arbitrator may have agreed the venue, date and time of the hearing with the parties, he should issue a formal notice to them giving this information and requiring them to acknowledge receipt of it. By this means he is able to ensure that there is no valid excuse for a party's absence: although if a party does not appear he should generally wait a reasonable period of time to allow for possible delays in travelling, before adjourning the hearing. In that event he should fix a new date and time for the hearing, notifying both parties as before, and adding the warning that in the event that either party fails to attend he will proceed with the hearing *ex parte* (see p. 16).

In arbitration the hearing is private; attendance is limited to the parties and their representatives and witnesses, the arbitrator and, where agreed by the parties, a legal adviser to the arbitrator and possibly a shorthand writer. Others may attend only with the consent of both parties and of the arbitrator, and usually such consent is given where a student wishes to attend, but not where the press or members of the public with no special interest apply to attend.

Where a question arises as to the credibility of one or more witnesses they may be excluded from the hearing until required to give their evidence.

THE HEARING

Courtesy

In a formal hearing the arbitrator may arrange for a member of his staff to ensure that both parties are present in the court room before he enters. In such a case those present rise when he enters, and sit only when invited to do so.

The arbitrator should be addressed as 'Sir' or, when referred to in the third person as 'The Arbitrator'—not as 'Mr Smith'.

Except while administering the oath, the arbitrator usually remains seated during the hearing. Counsel, solicitors and witnesses—again except while taking the oath—may also remain seated, although some counsel prefer to stand.

Challenges to jurisdiction

It may happen at the commencement of a hearing that a party challenges the arbitrator's jurisdiction as arbitrator. In such an event the arbitrator should hear the grounds upon which the challenge is based, and should ascertain why it is raised at this stage and not during the preliminaries. He should also provide an opportunity for the opposing party to make any submission that may be relevant to the matter. The arbitrator will then have to decide whether to proceed with the hearing, to adjourn it, or to abandon it altogether. Should he decide to proceed he will note the substance of the objection raised and advise both parties of his ruling, thereby leaving it open to the challenger to take further action should he so decide.

If the arbitrator thinks it prudent to adjourn the hearing while the challenge is investigated, he should warn the parties that taking this course will inevitably result in additional costs because of the time wasted by himself and by the parties and their representatives and witnesses; and that he will in due course award such additional costs having regard to the outcome of the challenge. Such a warning may, in cases where the challenge is of doubtful validity, result in its being abandoned.

Representation

The parties are free to choose the form of their representation, if any; they may appoint a layman, a technical advocate, a solicitor or counsel; but as explained in Chapter 5 they must make their intentions known to the other party.

If a party appears at the hearing with counsel without having given notice of that intention the arbitrator should invite the other party to apply for an adjournment to enable it to arrange similar representation if it so wishes. In such an event the additional costs resulting from the adjournment would be awarded against the party who failed to give notice.

Procedure

The arbitrator opens the hearing by reciting in outline the events that have led to it: the identity of the parties and of the contract between them, the arbitration agreement therein, the occurrence of a dispute, the manner of appointment of the arbitrator and his acceptance of that appointment. He then declares the hearing open.

The claimant's counsel or representative, or the claimant himself where not represented, opens his case by introducing himself and others of his party, and he may also introduce counsel for the defence where so represented. He proceeds by outlining the claimant's case, and then calling each witness in turn. Where, as is usual, evidence is to be given under oath or affirmation, the arbitrator will have prepared himself by having available a Bible, an Old Testament, and a card on which is typed the form of oath and of affirmation, as follows:

> 'I swear by Almighty God that the evidence I shall give touching the matters in dispute in this reference shall be the truth, the whole truth, and nothing but the truth.'

> 'I solemnly, sincerely and truly affirm and declare that I will true answers make to all such questions as shall be asked of me touching the matters in difference in this reference.'

Witnesses who are Christians should be required to stand and to swear upon the Bible, holding it in their right hand while taking the oath. Those of the Jewish faith should repeat the same words, holding the Old Testament. Others should be required to affirm by standing and repeating the words of the affirmation.

The sequence of giving evidence is firstly examination-in-chief by counsel for the witness's own party, cross-examination by the opposing counsel, and finally re-examination by the witness's own party. A witness of fact must not, as explained in Chapter 6, refer to notes while giving evidence, other than those made contemporaneously with the events he is describing. Should he refer to any written record the arbitrator should ask to see it and should allow the other party an opportunity to do so, to check that it is a genuine diary or other note made at the time.

A witness must not be 'led' during examination-in-chief or during re-examination: that is, he may not be asked questions which suggest their answer. He must not be asked 'was the concrete sloppy?' but may be asked 'what was the consistency of the concrete?' In practice, however, leading questions are usually permitted during examination-in-chief where they relate to matters that are not in contention: the identity of the witness, his appointment in his work and his presence on the site. This is simply to save time: it is quicker for counsel to obtain the answers he needs by asking: 'you are Joe Bloggs, you live at 25 High Street Blanktown, and you are employed as a site engineer by Bill Smith?' than to ask each of the questions that would otherwise be needed. The same principle is sometimes extended to other questions; but as soon as contentious matters are dealt with, the proper form of questioning must be used.

Usually the arbitrator will not object to the form of questioning where both parties are represented by lawyers, because they should be aware of the rules, and are free to object where necessary. Where the parties are not so represented however the arbitrator may require them to comply with the rules.

Leading questions may be asked during cross-examination: indeed they are often necessary, because one of the duties of cross-examining counsel is to put his version of events to witnesses called by his opponents. For example a witness for a contractor may be asked during cross-examination: 'I put it to you that the delays were not caused by late issue of the drawings, but by shortage of labour on the site?' It must be borne in mind that each witness will, or should, be called once only; that during that appearance he must be given the opportunity to comment upon the opposing party's version of the facts.

Questions during re-examination must be confined to matters that have been raised during cross-examination, usually with the object of correcting any misleading impressions that may have been given by the witness during that cross-examination. In the event that such re-examination strays— perhaps unintentionally—into matters that have not previously been raised, the opposing party's counsel would probably ask for, and be allowed, an opportunity to cross-examine on those new matters.

The arbitrator may ask questions of a witness at any time, but should preferably do so only at the conclusion of re-examination, in order not to interrupt the flow of evidence. Should he raise some fresh matter which either party considers to be misleading or to require further elucidation that party is generally allowed an opportunity to ask further questions.

Reference may be made, while taking oral evidence, to documents produced in evidence. Wherever possible such documents should have been agreed between the parties, copied and formed into bundles, each document being identified by a bundle letter and a number. In this way both parties and the arbitrator may refer without difficulty to such documents, or to items of real evidence. Similarly where figures have been agreed 'as figures' the agreement should have been put into writing and the letter incorporated in one of the agreed bundles.

Except where both parties have agreed to the making of a transcript of the hearing the arbitrator must rely upon his own notes, possibly supplemented by a tape recording. He will accordingly require evidence to be given sufficiently slowly to enable him to keep an adequate record. Where counsel are involved they wait until the arbitrator has finished writing his note of an answer before proceeding to the next question.

After each of the claimant's witnesses has given evidence-in-chief, has been cross-examined and re-examined, and has answered any questions the arbitrator may ask, that witness is allowed to stand down. The next witness is called and questioned in the same sequence, after having taken the oath, and this procedure is repeated until all of the claimant's witnesses have been called.

Counsel or other representative for the respondent is then invited to open his case, and may do so either by outlining the substance of the defence, or by calling his first witness. In many hearings the case for the defence will already have been made clear during cross-examination of the claimant's witnesses, so that an opening address may not be necessary.

Each of the defence witnesses is examined-in-chief, cross-examined and re-examined, and may be asked questions by the arbitrator, repeating the sequence of evidence for the claimant.

When all of the defence witnesses have given their evidence, the defence counsel or representative makes his closing speech, in which he emphasises the merits of his client's case and detracts from that of his opponent. Finally the claimant's counsel or representative makes his closing speech, again urging acceptance of his client's case.

It may sometimes happen that the respondent does not call any witnesses. In such a case the sequence of the hearing is varied in that the claimant's counsel is required to make his closing address before that of the respondent.

At the conclusion of the two closing addresses the arbitrator declares the hearing closed, and usually gives the parties an indication as to when his award will be published.

8. The Award

Synopsis
In making his award the arbitrator's objective is to define clearly, unambiguously, justly and enforcibly what the parties are to do and when they are to do it in order to resolve the matters in dispute. This chapter covers types, format and content of awards, and the manner in which their publication is notified to the parties.

Types of award
Unless otherwise stated, an award is final, and concludes the reference. Provision is however made in Section 14 of the 1950 Act for interim awards; and these are often used where certain matters need to be determined urgently, where determination of preliminary issues might save unnecessarily prolonged hearings, or where it is desired to deal separately with an award of costs (see Chapter 9).

Thus for example there may be a question whether a respondent is liable at all; if he is, the amount of that liability will have to be determined. In such a situation it may be sensible for the parties to agree, or in the absence of agreement for the arbitrator to direct, that the issue of liability be determined and made the subject of an interim award. Only if the respondent is found to be liable will it be necessary to determine the amount, or 'quantum' of that liability.

Again, although awards are usually made in monetary terms, there is provision in Section 15 of the 1950 Act for an arbitrator to order 'specific performance'—meaning in practical terms an award stating that a party shall perform certain specified works, or hand over specified goods or rights. The use of this provision requires great care, because of the risk that a further dispute may arise from an allegation that the work ordered to be done is not satisfactory; in general if work is alleged to be below the standard of workmanship provided by the terms of the contract it may well be that the second attempt to do the work may result in little improvement. Hence the general practice that specific performance should not be awarded where a monetary award would resolve the dispute in a satisfactory manner.

In exceptional cases—for example where both parties agree to an award of specific performance—the arbitrator should advise that the award should be interim only, with provision for making it final if and when the specified work has been satisfactorily completed. He should specify a reasonable period of time for completion of the work and require that after that period has expired both parties should confirm to him that the work has been satisfactorily completed, or should specify any defects that may be alleged. In the absence of agreement the arbitrator should inspect the work in the presence of both parties and make such final award (or possibly another interim award) as may be appropriate. Provision in such cases is often needed for extensions of the time for performing the work: for example if the contractor experiences delay in obtaining materials or from one of the causes that would have entitled him to an extension of time under the original contract.

Format of award

The main parts of an award are the headings, recitals, the operative part, date, signature and witness's signature. Where, as is becoming standard practice, reasons are given, they may be incorporated in the operative part or may be appended to the end of the award. Since the 1979 Act became law the practice of giving reasons in a separate document, and of specifying that they are not part of the award, is losing favour, because the danger that an award may be set aside or remitted because of an error on its face has been eliminated.

HEADINGS

Awards are headed with the standard introduction 'In the matter of the Arbitration Acts 1950–1979 and in the matter of an arbitration between . . .' followed by the full names of each party and the identification of the party as claimant or respondent. Where the arbitration is not conducted under the procedural law of England the Acts referred to should be those governing the procedural law applicable to the reference.

Beneath the names of the parties comes the heading 'Award'. Some

THE AWARD

arbitrators use the heading 'Final Award' but this is not strictly necessary because the award will be taken to be final unless otherwise described.

RECITALS

The word 'Whereas' is used to introduce a series of numbered paragraphs in which the arbitrator recites in sequence all of the steps that have led to his making the award. These commence with the identification and main purpose of the contract between the parties, the inclusion in that contract of an arbitration agreement and the manner in which the arbitrator is to be appointed, the occurrence of a dispute, the procedure and date of appointment of the arbitrator and the date upon which he accepted that appointment, an outline of the interlocutory stages including the dates of preliminary meetings and orders, reference to pleadings and to discovery of documents, and finally the dates and duration of the hearing. Where there have been any other events in the interlocutories, such as site inspections or interim awards or orders, these should be referred to in order to provide a full picture of the events that preceded the hearing.

It may in some cases be necessary to record other matters that may be relevant to the making of the award, such as special agreements as to procedure, as to whether or not reasons are required to be given in the award, or as to absence of a party from a meeting or from the hearing. The basic rule is that the recitals should be sufficient to show that the arbitrator has complied with the law in all of the matters that have led to the award.

THE OPERATIVE PART

Whether or not reasons are to be given in the award, the arbitrator must decide by a logical thought process what his award is to be, and this implies that he must set down his reasons in writing. Apart from the fact that so doing helps him to avoid any illogicality, he may find it necessary to refer to those reasons should any query arise from the award.

In the relatively short period that has elapsed since the 1979 Act became operative (on 1 August 1979) little authoritative guidance has emerged from the courts as to the form in which reasons should be given. Lord Justice Donaldson, President of the Chartered Institute of Arbitrators, suggested at the Institute's annual conference in November 1981 that arbitrators are not required to analyse the law. They should set down what happened—that is, their findings as to facts—and state their opinions as to the law applicable to those facts.

A full account of the facts must necessarily include events leading to the dispute, details of which are of course already well known to both parties. It has been suggested by some arbitrators that background details should be omitted, because in the majority of cases, in which there is no appeal from the award, the parties alone will read it, and they need not be told facts that they already know and are not in dispute. However the suggestion that such information should not be given unless and until required by the court (which has the power under Section 1(5) of the 1979 Act to order the arbitrator to state the reasons for his award in sufficient detail to enable the court to consider any question of law arising from it) was not approved by Lord Justice Donaldson, who urged that the background should always be included. In many cases such background need not add greatly to the length of the reasons, nor involve any great expenditure of the arbitrator's time.

In coming to his decisions on matters of fact—which include matters of opinion other than those relating to law—the arbitrator may use his expert knowledge of the matters in question in a general sense, but must not rely upon any special knowledge of the particular case without disclosing such knowledge to the parties. By so doing he gives the parties an opportunity to challenge his special knowledge and possibly to bring evidence refuting it or mitigating its effect. The point was clearly illustrated in *Fisher and Another* v. *P G Wellfair Ltd (1981)* in which the Court of Appeal, Lord Denning, Master of the Rolls, presiding, unanimously dismissed an appeal against a High Court order removing an arbitrator and setting aside his award because of his misconduct in using his special knowledge in forming a different view of the facts from that presented in evidence by expert witnesses, without providing an opportunity to deal with that different view. The case arose from defects in a block of flats, in respect of which the owners claimed £93,000 damages from the builders. The arbitrator awarded £13,000. Neither the builders, who were in liquidation, nor the NHBC who had guaranteed their performance, were represented at the hearing, at which experts of high repute gave evidence on behalf of the owners. In an affidavit the arbitrator had explained his understanding of his duty where a party was unrepresented to protect that party's interests: that is, to see that the claim was properly proved. He had listened carefully to evidence of fact from two witnesses and to four experts, and had intervened where clarification was required. But he had not considered it part of his duty to indicate at the hearing that he did not accept any particular evidence. Lord Denning did not accept that the arbitrator had a duty to protect an unrepresented party. Lord Justice Dunn, concurring, said that the arbitrator should not in effect give himself expert evidence or act on his own private opinion without signalling his intention to the parties.

If the arbitrator uses his expert knowledge in forming a view of the facts after the close of the hearing—for example where he calculates stresses or evaluates work after hearing the evidence— then it would appear sensible for him to notify both parties of the conclusions he has reached and to invite them to submit their representations and if necessary to apply for reopening of the hearing. Similarly if he foresees a need to make calculations or to use his expert knowledge in some such way after the hearing he could indicate this intention to the parties and ask if they agree to his doing so without reopening the hearing. Where the questions to be determined in this way are not of major importance it is the author's experience that such consent is usually given.

Having come to his decisions on matters of fact and of opinion—for example whether or not the physical conditions or artificial obstructions leading to a claim under Clause 12 of the ICE conditions could have been foreseen by an experienced contractor—the arbitrator has to form his opinions on any questions of law that arise from the facts found. Usually the question of law to be determined is whether or not a party to the dispute is in breach of contract, either in failing to pay to the contractor monies to which he is entitled, or in the contractor failing to execute work in accordance with the contract; and the answer to such questions is often evident from the facts found.

There are however cases in which the points of law may be far from simple: where for example a question arises as to a claim being barred under the Limitation Acts, or where the terms of a contract are not clear. In such cases the arbitrator may seek legal advice; if as suggested in Chapter 4 the arbitrator has included in the terms of his appointment, and has obtained the parties' agreement thereto, the power to obtain legal advice, he will not need any further authority. Alternatively, where the point of law is important, or is likely to affect future contracts he may think it preferable to obtain a decision from the High Court under Section 2 of the 1979 Act (see p. 31).

In reaching his decision whether or not to include reasons in his award, the arbitrator should respect the parties' wishes. If either party asks for reasons that fact should be recorded in the award and reasons should be given. The arbitrator should recognise that the request for reasons could lead to an appeal under Section 1 of the 1979 Act, in respect of which he may be called upon by the High Court to provide the more detailed reasons referred to on p. 46. Conversely if both parties agree that reasons shall not be given the arbitrator should comply; and it would be sensible for him in such circumstances to enquire if the parties wished to enter into an exclusion agreement under Section 3 of the 1979 Act, the effect of which would be to exclude the parties' rights to appeal to the High Court on a point of law.

Directions

Following the recitals and, where included, the reasons, the award continues by defining what is to be done to settle the dispute. The usual form of introductory wording, which is written in capitals, is: 'ACCORDINGLY I HEREBY AWARD AND DIRECT THAT,' after which the arbitrator sets down who is to pay what sum to whom, and when he is to do so, 'in full and final settlement of all claims (and counterclaims) referred to me.'

In addition to defining the sums to be paid in respect of the claims—which may be taken separately or lumped together as may be appropriate—the arbitrator must give his directions as to costs (see Chapter 9): which party is to pay the costs of the reference and the costs of the award, and the manner in which those costs are to be, or have been, determined. He must make provision for the possibility that the party who have paid his costs in taking up the award may not be the party directed in the award to bear such costs, by requiring the other party to reimburse the sum paid.

Finally the arbitrator should, where appropriate, mark the award 'Fit for Counsel' (see p. 24), sign it and have it witnessed.

Interest

Although there can be little doubt that an arbitrator is empowered to award interest on any sum payable by one party to the other the origin and extent of that power are at present matters of uncertainty.

Section 3 of the Law Reform (Miscellaneous Provisions) Act 1934 provides that a court may, if it thinks fit, order that there shall be '*included in the sum for which judgment is given* (my italics) interest at such rate as it thinks fit . . . for the whole or any part of the period between the date when the cause of action arose and the date of the judgment'. A problem arises from the strict interpretation of this section in that, where a claim is paid either immediately before an action begins or before an award is made, there is no principal sum with which the interest may be included, and therefore no interest may be paid. This was the essential point dealt with by the Court of Appeal in *Tehno-Impex* v. *Gebr van Weelde Scheepvaarkantoor BV* (1981), Lord Denning, Master of the Rolls, presiding, with Lord Justice Oliver and Lord Justice Watkins. The court declared unanimously that modern conditions with rapid changes in the value of money required an urgent reappraisal of the common law rule on interest, and by a majority decision, Lord Justice

Oliver dissenting, allowed an appeal from the arbitrator's award, upheld in the High Court, that no interest was due on money paid late by charterers to the owners in a maritime case. Leave to appeal to the House of Lords was granted.

Lord Denning took the opportunity to review the law concerning the award of interest by arbitrators and held that they have a wide discretion to award interest whenever it is just and equitable to do so. The power arises, he said, not from the 1934 Act but in equity: and they can award interest on interest. In expressing this opinion Lord Denning has, in the interests of justice, gone far beyond the limited power believed to be vested in arbitrators. But it is by no means clear that this statement was supported by Lord Justice Watkins, and quite clear that Lord Justice Oliver dissented. Hence it cannot be assumed that Lord Denning's expressions of views represent the law as it is. On the other hand his statement follows closely certain views expressed in the Law Commission's 'Report on Interest' published in June 1978, in which in paragraph 20 under the heading 'Aspects of the present law that are not in need of reform' appears the statement 'The equitable jurisdiction to award interest and to fix the rate at which it should be paid is extensive. It includes, for example, the power to order the payment of interest where money has been obtained or withheld by fraud or where it has been misapplied by someone in a fiduciary position. In such cases the court . . . may direct that such interest be compounded at appropriate intervals.' Thus it would appear that in Lord Denning's judgment commercial arbitrations are included in the categories to which the equitable jurisdiction applies. Whether or not the House of Lords will uphold this view, in Tehno-Impex or in some other case, remains to be seen.

Costs
The award should also include directions as to costs of the reference (that is, the parties' costs) and costs of the award (the arbitrator's costs). These subjects are dealt with in the following chapter.

Consent awards
Where, as sometimes happens, the parties negotiate a settlement of the matters in dispute between them, either during the interlocutory stages or during the hearing, it is often desirable that the terms of the settlement should be incorporated in an award made by the arbitrator in those terms, and called a consent award.

The purpose of such a document is to provide a means whereby the successful party may enforce the terms of the settlement just as any other award may be enforced (namely by application to the High Court for a judgment or order in the terms of the award, under Section 26 of the 1950 Act), and where necessary to enable costs to be taxed by the court (see Chapter 9).

Publication of the award

When it has been prepared, signed and witnessed, an award is said to be 'published'. Only the parties are entitled to see the award: hence the word 'published' does not have its usual meaning. There is however nothing to stop a party making the existence and content of the award known to the public if it so wishes, though such action is unusual.

The usual procedure adopted by the arbitrator in publishing his award is to write to both parties telling them that the award is available for collection at, or dispatch from, his office upon payment by either party of his charges, which he specifies in his letter. Upon receipt of payment from one party he hands or sends the award to that party, and simultaneously sends a signed copy of the award to the other party. The purpose of this procedure is of course to secure payment of his charges, it being probable that the party which is ultimately to bear those charges, namely the losing party, would be most reluctant to pay them. In many cases the charges are paid initially by the winning party, who then has to recover them from his opponent. This merely increases the sum payable by the loser to the winner, and does not, even where the award has to be enforced through the courts, necessitate a separate action in respect of the charges.

9. Costs

Synopsis
Wide powers to award costs and to determine their amount are vested in the arbitrator under Section 18 of the 1950 Act. But those powers must be used judicially: and where an unusual award of costs is made, reasons should be given.

1950 Act provisions
Section 18 of the 1950 Act provides that costs of the reference and award are in the discretion of the arbitrator, who may direct who shall pay those costs and may determine their amount.

The costs of the reference are the parties' costs, covering their legal representation, experts, witnesses' expenses, and any other costs incurred from the date of commencement of the arbitration until the end of the hearing. Costs of the award are the arbitrator's costs, i.e. his fees and expenses. Thus the Act empowers the arbitrator to determine the amount of his own charges, but a safeguard against the abuse of this power is contained in Section 19. Under that section an arbitrator who refuses to deliver his award except upon payment of his fees may be ordered to do so by the High Court, upon application by one of the parties and upon that party paying the sum demanded into court. The taxing master of the court thereupon taxes (that is, assesses) the amount of the arbitrator's fee, pays it to him and refunds the balance (if any) of the payment into court to the applicant. Where this procedure is used the arbitrator has the right to appear before the taxing master. A party which has agreed in writing to the arbitrator's fees in not entitled to use Section 19 of the Act.

Responsibility for costs

The basic rule used to determine who should pay the costs incurred in arbitration proceedings, as in the courts, is that 'costs follow the event'—meaning in general that the successful party should be awarded his costs. No difficulty arises in applying this rule in a simple case, where the claim either succeeds or fails in its entirety, and where there is no default on the part of the successful party.

In practice however complications often arise: for example a claim may succeed in part; or there may be a counterclaim which also succeeds wholly or in part; or the respondent may have made an offer which the claimant should have accepted; or costs may have been occasioned unnecessarily by the successful party. Arbitrators have often been criticised for their tendency to apportion costs in such cases; for example to award one half of the claimant's costs where only one of two claims succeeds.

The arbitrator should, it is suggested, base his award of costs upon his decision as to which party's action or inaction resulted in the costs being incurred, and should award costs against that party to the extent that they were necessary. Hence a party whose claim succeeds in part should be awarded costs, but omitting costs in respect of time spent unnecessarily, in pursuit of obviously invalid claims. Where there is a claim and a counter-claim, both of which succeed in whole or in part, the nett winner should be awarded his costs; but again to the extent that they were incurred necessarily. This follows from the fact that the nett winner had to proceed with the arbitration in order to obtain the nett sum to which he was found to be entitled.

Where one party makes an offer to settle the claims in a sum sufficient to cover the amount ultimately awarded by the arbitrator, plus costs incurred by the claimant up to the date of the offer, then the responsibility for the continuation of the dispute rests with the offeree, who should be made to bear costs incurred after the date of the offer.

Where a successful party is responsible for unnecessary costs—for example by failing to appear at meetings which have to be aborted, or by making late applications to amend pleadings, thereby increasing the costs of the hearing—that party should be made to bear all such unnecessary costs. This requirement is usually implemented by means of an order by the arbitrator, made at the time of the default, to the effect that the costs of the aborted meeting and the arbitrator's order shall be borne by the defaulting party 'in any event'—that is, irrespective of the outcome of the arbitration.

Offers to settle

It will be seen from the preceding paragraph that the making of an offer of sufficient magnitude to warrant its acceptance by the offeree protects the offeror against costs as from the date of the offer. The machinery whereby such offers may be made requires consideration.

(a) OPEN OFFERS

Either party may make an offer to settle to the other, by way of an 'open' letter (that is, a letter not marked 'without prejudice') which may therefore be produced in evidence. The disadvantage of this procedure to the offeror is that the letter might be interpreted by the arbitrator as an admission of liability notwithstanding that the offeror intends to contest liability if the arbitration proceeds.

(b) SEALED OFFERS

An offer may be made in a letter marked 'without prejudice', meaning that it is not an admission of liability: it does not prejudice the offeror's case, and cannot be given in evidence. In order that it may be effective it must however be brought to the arbitrator's notice before he deals with his award of costs, and this is done by the offeror or his representative handing a copy of the offer in a sealed envelope to the arbitrator, usually at the close of the hearing, with a request that he opens it after making his substantive award but before considering costs.

The disadvantages of this procedure are firstly that there will in such circumstances be no doubt in the arbitrator's mind that the envelope contains a copy of an offer. Hence to the extent that his award might have been influenced by the knowledge of an offer, he might still be influenced by the near certainty that an offer, albeit of unknown amount, was made. Secondly the fact that an offer was made does not necessarily mean that funds were available, and would have been paid, had the offer been accepted. Neither of these two disadvantages applies to the corresponding procedure in a civil action in court, in which the sum offered has to be paid into court, and neither the amount nor the existence of the offer is known to the judge until he comes to deal with costs.

(c) INTERIM AWARDS

The problem of dealing with offers arises in arbitration because, except in administered arbitrations, there is no 'court' into which payment may be made, or which can be made aware of the existence of the offer without its coming to the notice of the arbitrator. It is however possible for the arbitrator to notify to the parties his intention to make his substantive award in the form of an interim award, after publication of which he will hear the parties' representatives on the question of costs. In an important reference, or in any reference in which it appears likely that an offer may have been made, the arbitrator would be wise to adopt this procedure. It would of course be open to him to comply with their wishes if both parties request that the substantive award and costs are dealt with together. Where neither party makes such a request the arbitrator would not necessarily be correct in inferring that an offer had been made; it could be that the parties are unaware of the reason underlying his suggestion.

A party wishing to adopt this procedure, in a reference in which the arbitrator does not himself suggest it, could ask the arbitrator for an opportunity to address him on costs after his substantive award is published. Such a request is unlikely to be refused; indeed to do so might well provide grounds upon which the party making the request could obtain consent to appeal.

After having heard the parties' addresses on costs the arbitrator incorporates his orders as to costs in a final award, which is published in the usual way.

Failure to award costs

Provision is made in Section 18(4) of the 1950 Act whereby a party may, within 14 days of the publication of an award that fails to deal with costs, apply to the arbitrator for him to make an order directing by and to whom those costs shall be paid, and requiring the arbitrator, after hearing any party which may wish to be heard, to amend his award by adding directions as to costs. The procedure defined in this subsection appears to suit the requirements admirably, but strangely it is rarely used; possibly because an arbitrator who failed to deal with costs in his award might be thought to have done so inadvertently.

Taxation of costs

'Taxation' in relation to costs means 'determination of amount': the term is not related in any way to taxes as imposed by Inland Revenue. The arbitrator is empowered under Section 18(1) of the 1950 Act to 'tax or settle' both the costs of the reference and the costs of the award. Usually he taxes his own costs, because he is better able than anyone else to do so. He knows the time he has spent in dealing with the reference, and the rate per hour that is reasonable or has been agreed. He also knows what expenses he has incurred in travelling, in hiring accommodation for meetings, in taking advice, or in any other outgoing relating to the reference. Hence it would be absurd for him to ask that his own charges be taxed by a taxing master; although provision is of course available for such a course where a party considers the arbitrator's costs to be unreasonable (see p. 51). Where the arbitrator taxes his own costs, the form of wording used in his award is 'which I hereby tax and settle in the sum of £ . . .' thereby making it clear that he has exercised his powers under Section 18(1).

Conversely, in the case of costs of the reference—that is, the party's costs—the arbitrator is well advised not to use his powers to tax. Where the parties are legally represented, and especially where counsel are appointed, taxation may become complicated; and it is a subject better understood by lawyers than by most arbitrators.

The arbitrator should however determine the scale on which costs are to be paid by the party which is to bear them: such scales being:

(a) PARTY AND PARTY BASIS
'All such costs as were necessary or proper for the attainment of justice or for enforcing or defending the rights of the party whose costs are being taxed.' Costs that were incurred merely for convenience are disallowed on this scale, which is the usual scale in arbitration.

(b) COMMON FUND BASIS
This basis, which replaces 'costs as between solicitor and client' a scale authorised specifically in Section 18(1) of the 1950 Act, is more generous than party and party costs. It is defined as being 'the costs of all steps reasonably taken by a sensible solicitor in the interests of his client', and would normally apply only where an application is made to the High Court on a point of law.

(c) TRUSTEE BASIS
Formerly known as the 'solicitor and own client' basis, this scale is applicable only where a party to proceedings acts as a trustee or personal representative, the costs being paid out of the trust funds. This scale is not relevant to arbitration.

In almost every case in arbitration the arbitrator should award costs on a party and party basis, though he should leave it open to the parties to agree costs if they are able to do so. Hence the usual form of wording is to direct that 'the respondent shall bear the claimant's costs; such costs, if not agreed, to be taxed on a party and party basis'. If no scale is defined in the award the party and party basis will be assumed.

Avoiding unnecessary taxation

The arbitrator should recognise that taxation of costs can itself involve costs, and may be protracted. It follows that an award that obviates or minimises the need for taxation may be more sensible, and may do more good to the parties, than one based upon strict principles. For example where an offer deemed by the arbitrator to be acceptable was made at a date by which half of the total of costs had been incurred, strict application of the rules would lead to an award that the respondent bears the claimant's costs up to the date of the offer, and the claimant bears the respondent's costs thereafter. An order that each party bears its own costs, although not strictly accurate, is likely to be more beneficial to both parties in that it obviates the need for taxation.

Effect of taxation

One of the less equitable aspects of the law in relation to taxation of costs is that even where a party is found to be blameless in an arbitration, or in litigation, and is awarded costs, the sum allowed on taxation is almost invariably less—and often substantially less—than the costs actually incurred by that party. It is not within the power of the party in question, or the arbitrator, to correct this injustice. The party can however to some extent mitigate its loss by ensuring as far as possible that its costs fall within the definition of party and party costs; that is, that they are incurred necessarily.

Costs of the award

Whatever decision is reached by the arbitrator in relation to the parties' costs should apply equally to the arbitrator's costs: that is, the costs of the award. Thus the party found to be responsible for the other party's costs should also have to bear the arbitrator's costs. Where responsibility is allocated to one party up to a certain date and thereafter to the other, the arbitrator's costs for each period should be determined and awarded accordingly.

10. Finality of the Award; Enforcement; Appeals

Synopsis
Although the objective of arbitration is to produce an award which is just, final and enforceable, there are reasons why this objective is not always achieved. There may be accidental errors in, or omissions from, the award; it may have been procured improperly or it may contain errors of law. This chapter covers the enforcement of valid awards and the means by which erroneous awards may be rectified or nullified.

Enforcement
Where the losing party fails to honour an award, application may be made by the other party under Section 26 of the 1950 Act to the High Court for judgment in the terms of the award. Provided that the Court is satisfied that the award is valid judgment will normally be given, and the means of enforcement thereafter is similar to that of any other judgment of the High Court.

Correction of accidental errors
Although the arbitrator, having made and published his award, is *functus officio*—meaning that he has discharged his duty and therefore that his authority as arbitrator is ended—he is empowered under Section 17 of the 1950 Act to correct 'any clerical mistake or error arising from any accidental slip or omission'. It is rarely necessary in practice to invoke this power, because arbitrators should, and usually do, take great care to ensure that their awards do not contain mistakes or errors. The power given under this section cannot, of course, be used to correct other types of error, such as errors of law.

Amendments to deal with costs
Section 18(4) of the 1950 Act covers the situation where an award fails to deal with the costs of the reference. This provision is dealt with under Costs (p. 54).

Correction of errors of law
An arbitrator is judge of matters of fact and of matters of law. 'Fact' in this context includes opinion on technical matters but not on questions of law; 'law' covers the interpretation (or, in legal terminology, the 'construction') of a contract. The arbitrator's findings of fact are final in that they are not subject to any right of appeal, but his decisions on questions of law may, in certain circumstances, form the subject of an appeal to the High Court.

It is however open to both parties to enter into an agreement, after the dispute has arisen, excluding their right of appeal. Such an agreement is recognised under Section 3 of the 1979 Act and is termed an 'exclusion agreement'. Its effect is to make the arbitrator sole judge of questions of law; where the main concern of the parties is to reach finality an exclusion agreement, entered into at the commencement of the arbitration, will ensure that that aim is achieved.

Where no such agreement is in operation at the time of publication of the award Section 1 of the 1979 Act (which applies to all arbitrations commenced on or after 1 August 1979 and to other arbitrations where the parties agree that it should apply) provides a limited right of appeal from the arbitrator's decisions on questions of law. The intention of the Act however is to obviate what had become almost standard practice prior to its enactment, namely the pursuit of sometimes spurious 'points of law' through the hierarchy of the courts by means of the 'special case' procedure, which now no longer exists. The court will accordingly require to be satisfied that the question of law is a genuine and an important one, and may impose conditions upon the granting of leave to appeal.

A party wishing to appeal under this section of the 1979 Act must either obtain the consent of the other party to the reference, or must be given leave by the court. In most cases leave to appeal will be sought by a claimant whose claim has been disallowed, or by a respondent who has been found liable to the claimant; in both of these situations the successful party will almost certainly oppose any application to appeal. Hence in general the party wishing to appeal will have to apply for leave from the court.

In dealing with such applications the High Court requires to be satisfied that determination of the question of law could substantially affect the rights of one or more parties to the arbitration; leave to appeal, if granted, may be made subject to the applicant complying with such conditions as may be considered by the court to be appropriate. It is to be expected in general that such conditions will include the payment into court of any sum directed in the award to be paid; thereby ensuring that the applicant does not gain an advantage from postponement of the day of payment.

The practicalities of an appeal under the 1979 Act are closely related to the giving of reasons for the award, because where no reasons are given it may not be possible to determine whether or not the arbitrator has made an error of law. In its shortest form an award might consist of recitals followed by a direction as to payment by one party to the other: and unless there is some obvious error in such an award (for example, where a respondent has admitted liability for a sum greater than that awarded) such an award could not be challenged under this section of the 1979 Act.

One of the stated intentions of that Act is to encourage arbitrators to give reasons; but they are not required to do so. Furthermore, if both parties request that reasons be not given, then the arbitrator should respect that request. If reasons are required by one or both parties the arbitrator should usually comply, although he is not obliged to do so. Such a requirement, notified to the arbitrator before publication of his award, does however ensure that adequate reasons can be made available to the High Court if they are required in connection with an appeal.

Where the parties are content to rely upon the arbitrator's own decisions upon questions of law they may request that he does not give reasons in his award: alternatively or additionally they may enter into an exclusion agreement. Where rights of appeal are to be preserved the party or parties wishing to preserve them should require that reasons be given. Unless reasons are required by one of the parties before the award is made, or unless there are special reasons why reasons were not required, the High Court cannot order the arbitrator to give reasons. (Section 1(6) of the 1979 Act).

Appeals under Section 1 of the 1979 Act are dealt with in the Commercial Court of the Queen's Bench Division. Notice of appeal must be served within 21 days after publication of the award (RSC Order 73 Rule 5). Where leave to appeal is given the options open to the High Court on determination are to confirm, to vary or to set aside the award, or to remit it to the arbitrator for reconsideration, with the court's opinion on the question of law which was the subject of the appeal.

Misconduct by the arbitrator

Section 23 of the 1950 Act empowers the High Court to remove an arbitrator who misconducts himself or the proceedings. In such cases, or where it has been improperly procured, the award may be set aside by the court. A less severe remedy is available under Section 22 of the 1950 Act, which empowers the court to remit the matters referred, or any of them, to the arbitrator for reconsideration.

Where the award is set aside all of the proceedings that have led to it are null and void. The parties, if they wish to proceed with the arbitration, must appoint a new arbitrator and recommence the proceedings: hence many of the costs incurred in the aborted reference are likely to be repeated. On the other hand remission to the arbitrator for reconsideration is unlikely to result in any substantial delay or additional cost.

'Misconduct' in this context does not necessarily imply, although it includes, immoral behaviour. The use of the term is often criticised because it fails to distinguish between behaviour which is morally reprehensible and that which is merely mistaken, such as might result from inexperience. Examples of behaviour in the first category include the acceptance of bribes or other inducements to show favour to a party, corruption, fraud or dishonesty, or any form of bias induced by the arbitrator's relationship with or interest in a party. In the sense of mistaken behaviour misconduct includes unintentional failure to disclose a relationship with a party which is unlikely to influence the arbitrator's award, improper delegation of his duty, hearing inadmissible evidence or refusing to hear admissible evidence, hearing evidence in the absence of a party (except where the rules relating to *ex parte* proceedings have been observed), hearing or receiving any submission or communication from one party without the knowledge of the other, refusal to allow time for an application to the court on any matter in respect of which the parties have a right to apply, or the use of the arbitrator's expert or factual knowledge of matters at issue without advising the parties of his intention to do so or giving them an opportunity to challenge that knowledge.

The point at which an arbitrator's use of his own expert knowledge becomes misconduct may not always be clear. It is sometimes argued that the parties, having chosen their arbitrator partly or mainly because of his expert knowledge of the technical matters in dispute, should be able to rely upon his using that knowledge in determining those matters. In *Fisher and Another* v. *P G Wellfair Ltd (1981)* (see p. 46) Lord Denning gave the following guidance:

'He (the arbitrator) should use his special knowledge so as to understand the evidence that was given, but not to provide evidence on behalf of the defendants which they had not chosen to provide for themselves ... he should not use his knowledge to derogate from the evidence of the plaintiff's experts without putting his knowledge to them and giving them a chance of answering it and showing that his own view was wrong.'

In both of its forms misconduct covers any action contrary to the principles of natural justice, which require that no man may be a judge in his own cause, and that every party has a right to be heard and to challenge any statement or document prejudicial to its case.

Application under Section 23 of the 1950 Act for setting aside an award on the ground that it has been improperly procured is unlikely, because any allegation of illegality of the contract or of invalidity of the arbitration agreement in a contract is usually taken long before the arbitration reaches an award. Nevertheless the power is there for use in appropriate situations.

Where application is made under section 23 of the 1950 Act for removal of an arbitrator and for setting aside his award it is for the court to decide whether or not to allow the application, or to remit the award under Section 22. Generally the latter power is used where the matters referred are of a minor nature and as such are capable of being remedied by the arbitrator on having the defects pointed out to him. It is however recognised that the arbitrator, having committed himself to a view of the matters referred, may find it difficult to approach any question of that view with an entirely free mind. In such cases the court may feel obliged to adopt the more serious remedy of setting aside.

Matters which might be remitted include decisions upon interlocutory matters, such as granting or refusing applications for extensions of time or for the production of documents for which privilege is claimed, or defects in the award such as failure to deal with all of the matters referred to the arbitrator, or the inclusion of matters outside the reference.

Applications under Section 22 or 23 of the 1950 Act must be made within six weeks of the date of publication of the award. Where matters are remitted by the court to the arbitrator for reconsideration he must make his award within three months of the order, unless the order provides otherwise.

11. The Contractor as Claimant

Synopsis
Probably the most usual form of a contractor's involvement in arbitration is as claimant, where a dispute arises from rejection of his claims. This chapter examines the origin of such disputes and ways in which they may sometimes be avoided. It also seeks to define the action that should be taken by a competent contractor: firstly to minimise the likelihood of his having to invoke arbitration; and secondly, where it is unavoidable, to ensure that the case he presents is valid and convincing. That action commences with the preparation of the tender.

The tender
A contract is created by a valid acceptance of a valid offer. Certain other elements must also be present: there must be consideration, an intention to create a legally-binding relationship, and certainty; but these are usually adequately covered in the offer, which in construction parlance is the tender.

Whether or not the tender documents issued by the employer so provide, the tenderer may limit the validity of his tender to a stated period of time. If by so doing he contravenes a requirement of the employer, then the courses open to the employer are to waive that requirement, to negotiate for its removal, or to ignore the tender. In any event, and notwithstanding any undertaking he may have given, the tenderer may at any time *prior to its acceptance* withdraw the tender.

If the tenderer neither limits the period of validity of his tender nor withdraws it, then it remains open for acceptance within a 'reasonable' period of time: the question 'what is reasonable?' being one for decision by the courts in the event of a dispute.

In order to safeguard himself the tenderer should withdraw any tender that has not automatically lapsed through a time limit, when he no longer wishes it to be accepted: otherwise he may receive an unwelcome reminder, in the form of an acceptance, that the tender is still valid. If the tenderer wishes to challenge the validity of the acceptance on the ground that it has not been issued within a reasonable time he should give notice to that effect immediately, and should not take any step that might imply his acceptance of the existence of a contract. It is too late, at this stage, to demand an increase in the tender sum to take account of inflation, although such an increase could possibly be negotiated with an employer who accepts the tenderer's contention that because of the passage of time the tender has lapsed. If the tenderer merely accepts the existence of the contract created by acceptance, however late, of his tender, then it is useless to claim at some later date that he is entitled to compensation in respect of the delay, unless such a provision is already built into the contract as a 'variation of price' clause.

In preparing the tender the contractor should remember that in the event of a dispute arising, for example from a varied quantity or type of work, the basis upon which the work included in the tender was priced will almost certainly be relevant, and pricing notes may have to be produced on discovery (see p. 27). For this reason the estimator's notes should be clear, logical and legible: especially where, for example, the make-up of an item includes a fixed sum in addition to a rate related to the quantity. In such a case the contractor is entitled to, and must be able to justify, an enhanced rate should the quantity be reduced. Conversely, where the pricing of an item depends upon the availability of a limited quantity of material, such as filling, at a cheap price, an *increase* in the quantity required by the employer may justify an enhanced rate. The apparent illogicality of the contractor's seeking an enhanced rate in both of these instances of variation may not be readily acceptable to the employer or to his engineer: it is only by making available pricing notes and evidence in support of them, such as quotations, that valid claims of this nature may be established.

Again, the contractor should ensure that his methods and construction programme are clearly defined and are available for reference in the event of a dispute. In some cases it may be desirable, where the construction methods or programme have an important effect on the amount of the tender, to include the method statement or programme as part of the tender documents: otherwise the contractor could find himself in the position of having his tender accepted and his method or programme later disapproved.

This situation may arise where a tenderer wishes to complete the work in less than the time allowed for it in the tender documents, in order to reduce his oncosts. A proposal based on such a reduction often incurs a suspicion that it presages a claim for delay, and may therefore be rejected by the employer if it appears after the contract has been made. By submitting his construction programme with the tender, and making it clear that the tender is conditional upon that programme being approved, the contractor obviates this possible source of dispute.

Where the tenderer finds it necessary to qualify his tender he should ensure that the qualification is clearly defined and that it is *incorporated in the tender*. A tenderer who submits a tender on the form provided, and submits qualifications in a separate covering letter to which no reference is made on the form of tender, runs the risk that the tender may be accepted as a separate document, and the covering letter ignored.

The acceptance

The other main element needed to create a contract is a valid acceptance: that is, an acceptance given during the period of validity of the offer, and in terms compatible with that offer. A simple statement 'I hereby accept your offer' is sufficient, provided of course that there is enough information to identify the offer to which it relates. If the 'acceptance' is not in terms compatible with the offer then it is not an acceptance at all, but a counter-offer, which requires acceptance by the other party before a contract can come into existence.

For example the acceptance of a qualified tender, subject to the removal of the qualifications, is a counter-offer which the tenderer may accept. Alternatively he may possibly agree to remove the qualifications subject to an increase in the amount of the tender; thereby making a further counter-offer, which requires acceptance by the employer if a contract is to be formed. In this way there may be a series of offers and counter-offers: and it is only when the terms of an acceptance are compatible with the last counter-offer that a contract comes into being. There is however a danger that a party to such a series of counter-offers may find itself deemed in law to have accepted the last offer made. This may happen where a tenderer, having received a counter-offer, starts work on the site: such an action usually constitutes an implied acceptance of the last offer made: and even if the contractor makes it clear, before starting, that he is doing so pending agreement of the outstanding issues, such action is unlikely to help his

THE CONTRACTOR AS CLAIMANT

contentions. For this amounts to an agreement to agree, which for obvious reasons is not enforceable in law.

Similarly an employer who instructs a contractor to start work is likely to be deemed to have accepted the tender and so to have created a contract.

Letters of intent

The usual objective of a letter of intent is to allow preliminary work to proceed while formalities such as financial or planning approvals are obtained. The form of wording may be '. . . it is the Council's intention to enter into a contract when . . . and meanwhile the Council has no objection to your ordering materials/designing the temporary works/erecting site offices . . .' or whatever preliminary activity may be intended. Unfortunately for the contractor a letter in this form does not constitute an acceptance of his tender: neither does it entitle him to any payment in the event that the contract does not materialise for any reason. The contractor should therefore be quite clear that if he starts work on receiving such a letter he will receive neither payment nor any compensation should the contract not come into being. These risks are his. If he wishes to avoid such risks he must require, as a condition of his starting on the preliminary work, that the employer undertakes to pay the cost of that preliminary work in the event that the contract does not come into being.

The contract

'Unless and until a formal Agreement is prepared and executed this Tender, together with your written acceptance thereof, shall constitute a binding Contract between us.'

The quotation, from the Form of Tender included in the ICE Conditions of Contract, merely sets out what is in any case the position in law. It follows that the question whether or not a formal agreement should be entered into and signed—and possibly sealed—by both parties is of little significance, since a perfectly adequate contract exists from the time of acceptance of the contractor's tender. The parties should however ensure that, where a formal agreement is made, it incorporates everything that has been agreed by the parties during any negotiations that may have taken place between the submission of the tender and the letter of acceptance. This it may do either by reference to letters between the parties setting out the agreed terms, or by a separate statement of the points that have been agreed during the negotiations. In any case the formal agreement, if made, should have annexed to it the tender drawings and any other information such as site investigation records made available to tenderers, the tender and all supporting documents, and the letter of acceptance.

The contract, whether in the form of the original tender and the letter of acceptance with appendices to those documents, or whether as a formal agreement, defines what is to be constructed and when it is to be completed: how much money is to be paid by the employer to the contractor, and the rights and obligations of each party in relation to the other. As such it is of vital importance in the determination of any dispute that may later arise, because the origin of any such dispute must lie in an allegation that some change has been made: either in the nature and/or quantity of the work to be performed, or in the way the contractor has performed it.

The construction period

Probably the most important single factor in ensuring that the contractor does not suffer unnecessarily from unforeseen difficulties, delays or alterations ordered during the course of the work is his maintenance of adequate records during the period of construction. The nature of civil engineering work is such that in almost every contract alterations in the work or in the manner or sequence of its construction must be expected. Ground conditions may not be as foreseen or as indicated by the borings and trial holes; weather conditions may be unfavourable; and alterations to the work may be needed in order to cope with the unexpected, to accommodate changes in the employer's requirements, to take advantage of changing technologies, or to correct errors in the design. All of these factors, together with the engineer's actions or omissions in his administration of the contract work may give rise to variations, delays or disruptions of the work: and it is only by maintaining full and accurate records of these matters and events as they occur that the contractor can hope to obtain proper recompense for their effect on the costs he incurs.

In most civil engineering contracts the contractor's records should include:
  (a) Site diaries, in which are recorded the weather, the state of progress on each item of work, and the causes of any delays being encountered in any part of the work;
  (b) Progress charts, which in the case of underground work may include records of subsoil strata, water levels and so on;
  (c) Programmes of future work, including a dated copy of each revision of the programme;
  (d) Details of all plant and labour employed on site, and of their allocation to various parts of the project, including cost information;

THE CONTRACTOR AS CLAIMANT 67

(e) Details of site oncosts: supervisory and non-productive labour, office costs including telephone, heating, cleaning etc; site workshops and mess-rooms; sanitation; water supply; site transport; small tools; insurances; watching and lighting;

(f) Records of lump-sum costs incurred in establishing and in dismantling the site, such as costs of transporting plant to and from the site, erection of offices and sheds and constructing access roads.

(g) All correspondence with the employer, engineer and engineer's representative. This should include variations, instructions, amended drawings; the contractor's confirmation of oral instructions given by the engineer or by his representative, and the contractor's notifications to the engineer of information required or of any other matter causing or likely to cause delay to the progress of the works.

(h) Correspondence with other parties, such as subcontractors, suppliers and any other organisations or persons who may be involved in the provision of goods or services required in connection with the works.

It should be recognised that the major element of most claims arising from civil engineering contracts is the cost of labour, plant and site oncosts during periods of delay. Hence it is important to the contractor that he should be able to produce evidence as to the causes of any delays suffered, of his having notified the engineer of those causes, and the effects of the delays in terms of additional costs. He should also ensure, as far as may be practicable, that notices are served as laid down in the contract. Failure to serve such notices may not be fatal to claims, but may well give grounds for a contention by the employer that he was thereby precluded from taking avoiding action, or that he was unable to check and record costs resulting from the delay.

Claims

Where it appears to the contractor that he is entitled to be paid some additional money in respect of additional costs incurred by him, he should set out the facts giving rise to the claim, identify the clause of the contract entitling him to payment, and calculate the amount of the claim, including where appropriate allowances for oncosts and for profit. In general such a claim should be lodged as soon as possible after the events from which it originates but, where necessary, information should be given piecemeal, as it becomes available. For example, where the whole or any **part** of the works is held up because of lack of information, notice should be given of the need for such information as soon as the contractor becomes aware of the deficiency; information as to the delay suffered and the resulting costs can then be given as the extent of the delay, and its likely effects on the remainder of the work, become known.

When all information needed by the engineer to ascertain the validity and the evaluation (or 'quantum') of the claim has been submitted, the contractor is entitled to expect that it will be dealt with, so that any sum to which the contractor is found to be entitled may be included in a certificate as soon as may be practicable. It is to be expected that the engineer may require a reasonable period of time for his consideration of the basis and evaluation of the claim; the question of what is reasonable depending upon the circumstances and the complexity of the claim. In most cases it should be possible for him to reach a decision within a month or two of his receiving full details, and where, because of the continuing nature of the additional costs or for any other reason, it is not possible to arrive at a final valuation the engineer should be willing to certify an appropriate payment on account. Certainly there is no excuse for any suggestion that claims should be considered after all of the work has been completed: indeed any question as to the validity of the claim should be raised immediately, so that it may be dealt with while the facts are fresh in the minds of those involved, and while, where necessary, subsoil or other information having a bearing upon the claim may be ascertained and recorded.

One of the difficulties facing the engineer in considering the contractor's claims is that he is called upon to play two quite different, and sometimes conflicting, roles. He must represent the interests of the employer, his client, of whom he is a paid agent; simultaneously he must act in a quasi-judicial capacity in maintaining a fair and impartial balance between the interests of the employer and of the contractor. In some cases that difficulty may be enhanced by the knowledge that his own actions as engineer under the contract may have given rise to the claim as, for example, where the contractor alleges that delay has been caused through late issue of working drawings.

During the course of the engineer's consideration of a claim the contractor should of course provide any additional information that the engineer may reasonably require: and he should recognise that in the event of his having to invoke arbitration, full details of the contractor's pricing or other relevant information will have to be produced on discovery. There is nothing to gain by any claim that the contractor's pricing details are 'confidential': although he may reasonably expect the engineer to preserve that confidentiality so far as may be consistent with his having access to all relevant information.

Disputes

If the engineer fails to deal with the claims within a reasonable time, or rejects them in whole or in part, the contractor may (i) accept that action or inaction; (ii) seek an opportunity to persuade the engineer to reconsider the claims or to reverse his decision; (iii) give notice that a dispute has arisen. Usually it is unwise for the contractor to take the third course until he is sure that there is nothing to gain by further discussion for although invoking the dispute procedure under Clause 66 of the ICE Conditions, or corresponding clause of another form, does not preclude further discussion, it limits the time available for such discussion.

Where after due consideration the contractor decides to invoke Clause 66 he should write to the engineer requiring him to give his decision under that clause on the matters in difference, sending his letter by recorded delivery as a precaution against any possible future allegation that the notice was not received. At the same time the contractor should note in his diary the day on which three months will have elapsed from the date of service of the notice.

During this first period of three months the contractor should continue to provide any further information the engineer may require, and should attend for discussions of the claim if called upon to do so. After the period has elapsed, or upon receipt of the engineer's decision under Clause 66 if this arrives earlier, the contractor may, if dissatisfied with that decision, give notice of arbitration. Such notice must be given either where the engineer fails to reply to the original notice, before six months have elapsed from that notice, or where the engineer does reply within the first period of three months, within a period of three months from the date of the reply notifying the engineer's decision.

Clause 66 of the ICE Conditions seeks to postpone any reference to arbitration until after completion—or alleged completion—of the works. Provision is however made in Clause 66(2) for immediate arbitration in the case of a dispute arising under Clause 12 of the Conditions (unforeseeable physical conditions or artificial obstructions) or from the withholding by the engineer of any certificate. The second of these two provisions will in many cases open the door to immediate arbitration of any rejected claim. In *A E Farr Ltd* v. *Ministry of Transport (1960)* it was held by Lord Denning in the Court of Appeal that failure by the engineer to certify payment of more than £15,000 of a proper claim of £20,000 constituted the withholding of a certificate. The question whether or not a similar ruling would have applied to a dispute relating to measurement as distinct from a claim remains open, there being no authority on this point. Nevertheless it is clear that a right to immediate arbitration exists in respect of any substantial claim; and it may apply equally to a measurement dispute.

Before embarking upon an 'immediate' arbitration however the contractor should consider whether or not this is in his best interests. The purpose of the clause 66 limitation of immediate arbitration, albeit that it is largely ineffective, is to ensure that as far as is possible all matters in dispute are dealt with in a single arbitration, which must of necessity be deferred until work has been completed. In this way costs should be kept to a minimum. Conversely, if the contractor seeks to refer each dispute to arbitration as it arises, the total of costs incurred in the series of arbitrations that might result is likely to be substantially greater than those of a single reference covering all of the disputed items. In his award of costs the arbitrator should have regard not only to the outcome of the claims: he should also consider whether or not the costs were necessary. Hence, unless satisfied that the contractor had no option but to refer each matter separately—for example for reasons of cash flow—he would in such circumstances award costs, or a major part of them, against the contractor, even where the claims succeed.

Selection of the arbitrator

As has been explained in Chapter 4, the contractor may sometimes be able to influence the choice of arbitrator, in that he may put forward one or more nominees for the employer's agreement: he may, where the employer makes counter-nominations, either agree to one of the nominees or reject them all; and he may, where it becomes necessary to apply for an appointment by the President of the ICE or other appointing authority, suggest appropriate qualifications for the arbitrator.

It is of course fundamental that the arbitrator must be utterly impartial, and in putting forward nominees the contractor should observe this requirement strictly. The other basic requirements of the arbitrator are that he must have a general technical knowledge of the subject matter of the dispute, but no knowledge of the particular dispute, and he must have judicial capacity.

Additionally it is desirable from both parties' viewpoints that he should be knowledgeable and experienced in arbitration procedure and law, and, from the viewpoint of the contractor in particular, that he should have knowledge and understanding of the business of contracting.

Much detailed information as to these attributes is available in the List of Arbitrators, published by the Institution of Civil Engineers and available from the Arbitration Officer of that Institution for a small charge.

In assessing a candidate's knowledge of arbitration account should be taken not only of the statement of arbitration experience included in the list: the question whether or not the person is a Fellow of the Chartered Institute of Arbitrators is also relevant. For it is reasonable to assume that a person who is a Fellow of the CIArb recognises arbitration as a subject worthy of study as a separate discipline, and that he has attained a standard of knowledge recognised by the Institute as being appropriate to one seeking appointment to be an arbitrator. Conversely the appointment of an arbitrator who is not adequately trained in arbitration is likely to lead to additional costs and delays, while that person seeks advice on procedure or on legal questions that may arise during the reference, the answer to which would be known by an experienced arbitrator.

Where attempts by the parties to agree upon an arbitrator prove unsuccessful the contractor should ensure, when applying for an appointment by the President, that full information as to the matters in dispute is given on the application form, to assist him in making an appropriate choice. Where, for example, the dispute relates to the pricing of varied work, it is to be hoped that the arbitrator appointed will have experience in such matters: preferably as a contractor.

The preliminaries

The main objectives of the claimant—in this case the contractor—are to obtain full recompense for the losses he has suffered, including the costs he incurs in obtaining that recompense, and to do so within as short a period of time as may be practicable. The first of these objectives is achieved by thorough preparation and presentation of the claimant's case, and the second may to a large extent be influenced by the claimant's action in setting the pace.

If, as sometimes happens, no communication is received from the arbitrator for a week or two after his appointment, the claimant should take the initiative by writing to him requesting him to convene a preliminary meeting as soon as possible, and putting forward up to say 10 dates upon which the claimant would be able to attend. A copy of this letter, and indeed of all letters sent to the arbitrator, should be sent to the respondent, the original being marked to show that the copy has been sent. If the claimant is able he may offer to make available a suitable venue for the preliminary meeting, having regard to the convenience of the arbitrator and of the respondent. The claimant should however make it clear that the offer is made only in an attempt to be helpful, and that he is quite willing to attend at whatever venue may be chosen by the arbitrator.

If for any reason it appears inappropriate to suggest a meeting—for example where the sum in dispute is so small as not to warrant the costs involved—the contractor may write to the respondent suggesting a draft Order for Directions (see SD/12) for his agreement. If the respondent does agree, then the claimant may send a copy of the draft, and of the respondent's letter of agreement, to the arbitrator, requesting him to make the order by consent.

Where a preliminary meeting is held one of its main purposes is to define a timetable for the several stages of the interlocutory proceedings. The claimant should estimate in advance of the meeting how long he requires for preparation of his Points of Claim, bearing in mind that whatever time he requires will to some extent form a yardstick by which the respondent will request and the arbitrator will allow time for the Points of Defence. The respondent will probably argue in any case for a longer period of time than that allowed for the claim, on the ground that the claimant has been able to commence his drafting of the Points of Claim whenever he chose to do so, while the respondent must await receipt of that document before he can start to draft his defence. However in the case of disputes referred to arbitration under clause 66 of the ICE Conditions it may usually be argued by the claimant that the respondent is already aware of the substance of the claims, which must already have been submitted to the engineer under the first stage of the clause 66 procedure.

If the respondent requests what appears to the claimant to be an excessive period of time for preparing the defence he may request that the arbitrator reduces it to a reasonable period: but pressing such an argument too far may be inadvisable, because it may lead to requests at a later date for extensions of time.

In most cases where there is a counterclaim the claimant will be aware of its existence and substance before the preliminary meeting, and should therefore be able to estimate what period of time he will require for preparing his defence to it.

Points of reply must be confined to dealing with any fresh matter raised in the defence, and therefore should not take long to prepare, if indeed they are needed at all. In many cases a period of two weeks is ample.

Time can often be saved by the parties' preparing their lists of documents concurrently with the final stages of the pleadings. Usually by that time it has become clear which documents are relevant to the matters at issue, and it is therefore not unreasonable to suggest that lists of documents are exchanged not later than the date fixed for the delivery of the points of reply.

Progress with the interlocutory proceedings is often delayed by requests for extensions of time. The claimant should, wherever possible, avoid having to ask for extensions, not only because of the delay they may, if granted, cause directly, but because of their effect in implying an entitlement of the respondent to a similar or perhaps longer extension. Usually the arbitrator will grant a first request, if reasonable in amount and soundly based, but in the case of subsequent applications by the same party he should generally seek the observations of the opposing party before determining the application, and should where appropriate do so at a meeting convened for that purpose. It often happens that the respondent, having no incentive to expedite the proceedings, seeks to delay them in every way open to him; and where the claimant becomes aware of that strategy he should if necessary draw it to the arbitrator's attention. The respondent in that situation will of course readily agree to any application by the claimant for an extension of time and will quote the extension given as a reason why he himself should be granted a similar or longer extension. Where the claimant wishes to oppose an application by the respondent for an extension, and where he can reasonably do so, he may request that the arbitrator hear his objections to the application at a meeting: and he may request a meeting in a case where the respondent has overrun the time allowed him for delivery of pleadings or other documents. In either of these situations the claimant may reasonably expect, and should request, that the arbitrator awards costs in his favour in any event: that is, whatever the outcome of the claims.

Another potential source of delay during the interlocutory proceedings is the possibility of requests for Further and Better Particulars. These can best be avoided by the claimant by ensuring that his Points of Claim are fully detailed, and that they do not include any vague allegations: for example that the engineer ordered 'numerous' variations, or that he failed on 'several' occasions to reply to the claimant's request for information. Such expressions invite a request for details of all of the variations alleged to have been ordered, and of each and every occasion upon which the contractor requested, but did not receive, information. By foreseeing such requests for particulars, and by including them in the original pleadings, the scope for delaying tactics may be restricted.

On the other hand the contractor must ensure that he has all the particulars that may be needed in refuting any allegations in the defence. Where for example there is an allegation that the works were delayed, not by a failure by the engineer to provide working drawings but by insufficiency of plant and labour on the site, the contractor should ensure that he has full records of the plant used, with dates of arrival on and departure from the site of each item, and the numbers of each category of labour on site during each week of the contract period. Where such matters are likely to be relevant, the claimant should summarise the information and request that the respondent agree it, having examined the original records from which it is extracted. In this way unnecessary and expensive delays during the hearing, while details are checked, may sometimes be avoided.

Another important part of the preliminaries is that of discovery, in that it provides an opportunity to ascertain the truth. The contractor should ensure that all documents likely to be relevant are produced, subject only to the limitation of privilege where relevant. For example where a subcontractor is in dispute with the main contractor, correspondence between the main contractor and the engineer or the employer may be very relevant to any allegation of defects in the subcontractor's work, and to any allegation by the subcontractor that his claims have not been adequately presented to the employer.

The hearing

In his preparations for the hearing the contractor should study the pleadings carefully to determine the precise points at which issues arise, and should prepare his evidence to prove those issues. Much valuable time is saved at the hearing by omitting any matter that is not in contention, except as may be needed to form a background to the matters in dispute. He can then concentrate his attention on the matters he has to prove, and ensure that adequate evidence is available on each such matter.

Documentary evidence carries more weight than evidence given orally, because it is not subject to the vagaries of memory or to deliberate distortion. Where credibility is likely to be in issue, the contractor should if necessary request that the arbitrator takes evidence on oath—which he should generally do without prompting from a party—and he may where necessary go further, in deciding to be represented in such cases by counsel. This is because counsel's skill in cross-examination may be invaluable in ascertaining the truth where witnesses are suspected of being unreliable. Again, the appointment of counsel may be wise in cases where difficult questions of law arise. In many cases however the issues that arise are mainly of a technical nature, and as such may be better presented to the arbitrator by a witness or by an advocate who understands those technicalities.

At the conclusion of the hearing the contractor should carefully consider whether to request that the arbitrator gives, or does not give, reasons in his award, having regard to the considerations referred to in Chapter 10.

THE CONTRACTOR AS CLAIMANT

Where it appears likely that the arbitrator will make decisions favourable to the contractor on questions of law that arise, or where the contractor's primary objective is finality, he may request that reasons should not be given, but to be effective such a request would have to be agreed to by the respondent. Conversely, where the contractor thinks it possible that the arbitrator may make an error in law that favours the respondent he should request the arbitrator to give reasons.

Offers

At any stage during the proceedings the respondent may make an offer to settle the claims. Besides his consideration of the acceptability of that offer, the contractor should consider the significance of it as a factor influencing the award of costs. He should form an assessment of the value of the claims in total, having regard to the probability of success in the case of each item, and the likely award against that item if it succeeds. Where the offer made is in excess of the evaluation of claims made in this way, and taking account of costs incurred up to the time of the offer, then the contractor should accept the offer: otherwise he incurs the very real risk that, should the arbitrator award a lower sum, he may order the contractor to bear both parties' costs and the costs of the award—that is, the arbitrator's charges.

Where the contractor prefers to gamble upon being awarded a higher sum by the arbitrator, or where he thinks it likely that the respondent may increase his offer, he may of course reject an offer that appears to be in his favour. Alternatively, where there are a number of items in the claim, he may request that the respondent makes a specific offer against each item, in the hope that agreement can be reached on some of the claims, leaving the others to be dealt with by the arbitrator.

Upsetting the award

Where the claimant believes that the award is wrong in law, or that the arbitrator has misconducted himself or the proceedings he may, subject to the limitations referred to in Chapter 10, initiate proceedings for an appeal for remission or setting aside of the award. Such action, which must be taken in the High Court and which of necessity requires the appointment of counsel, is beyond the scope of this introductory volume.

Appendix A. Specimen Documents

SD/1 Application for a stay of court proceedings
    2 Request for engineer's decision under Clause 66 of the ICE Conditions
    3 Notice of arbitration under ICE Conditions
    4 Notice to concur under ICE Conditions
    5 Application to the President of the ICE for appointment
    6 Notice of arbitration and notice to concur—general
    7 Application to the President to appoint—general
    8 Notice of appointment—general
    9 Notice of appointment where parties are not represented
   10 Notice of appointment—small claim; parties not represented
   11 Check list for preliminary meeting
   12 Order for directions
   13 Points of Claim
   14 Points of Defence
   15 Points of Reply
   16 Request for further and better particulars of the points of Claim
   17 Further and better particulars of the points of Claim
   18 Scott Schedule
   19 List of documents
   20 Proof of evidence
   21 Award
   22 Notice of publication of award

SD/1 Application for a stay of court proceedings

IN THE HIGH COURT OF JUSTICE
QUEEN'S BENCH DIVISION

1982 W No 1234

BETWEEN:

                Wright, Charlie & Company   PLAINTIFFS

                            and

           The Universal Construction Company Ltd   DEFENDANTS

1. This is an Application by The Universal Construction Company Ltd, Defendants named in the above action, for a stay of proceedings under Section 4 of the Arbitration Act 1950.

2. The matters in dispute arise from a Contract in writing between the parties, dated 25 June 1981.

3. The said Contract contains, in Clause 18 thereof, a provision that if any dispute arises between the parties in connection with the Contract, it shall be referred to the arbitration and final decision of a person agreed between the parties, or failing such agreement, appointed upon the application of either of the parties by the President for the time being of the Institution of Civil Engineers.

4. We have entered an appearance to the writ in this action and have a good defence thereto.

5. At the date when the action was commenced we were, and we so remain, ready and willing to do all things necessary to the proper conduct of the arbitration, in accordance with the provisions of the said Contract.

Dated this Fourteenth day of February 1982

Joe Bloggs

Joe Bloggs
for and on behalf of the Universal Construction Company Ltd

SD/2 Request for engineer's decision under Clause 66 of the ICE Conditions

From: The Universal Construction Company Ltd
To: Messrs I K Brunel & Partners

1st October 1980

Dear Sirs

<u>Construction of M100 Motorway: Contract No 6</u>

We hereby give notice that a dispute has arisen from the above contract, as a consequence of your failure to certify payment of the sums due to us in respect of claims totalling £96 000 in value, details of which were notified to you on 29th May 1980.

We now request your decision, under Clause 66 of the contract, as to whether or not you will certify payment of the sums in dispute.

Yours faithfully

for The Universal Construction Company Ltd

Joe Bloggs

J Bloggs
Director

SD/3 Notice of arbitration

Form ArbICE issued by **The Institution of Civil Engineers**
Great George Street London SW1P 3AA
Telephone: 01-222 7722 Telegrams: Institution London SW1

Part 1: DISPUTE(S) OR DIFFERENCE(S) TO BE REFERRED TO ARBITRATION in accordance with Clause 66 of the ICE Conditions of Contract

IN THE MATTER OF AN AGREEMENT of which the ICE Conditions of Contract [1] ~~Fourth Edition (January 1955)~~ [1] Fifth Edition (June 1973) forms part and which was made the **Second** day of **January** 19 **79** between: **Wessex County Council**

who is referred to in the Agreement as the Employer and whose address is: **County Council Offices Thomas Hardy Road   Wiltonbury   Wessex**

of the one part and: **The Universal Construction Company Ltd**

who is referred to in the Agreement as the Contractor and whose address is: **Construction House Telford Road   Basingshot   Hampshire**

of the other part for the construction of certain Works namely: **M100 Motorway: Contract No 6 (Bridge over River Avon)**

AND IN THE MATTER OF DISPUTE(S) OR DIFFERENCE(S) which was (were) referred to the Engineer in accordance with Clause 66 of the ICE Conditions of Contract in letter(s) from: **The Universal Construction Company Ltd** dated: **1st October 1980**

[1] and to which notice of the Engineer's decision in accordance with Clause 66 of the ICE Conditions of Contract was given in the Engineer's letter(s) to: **The Universal Construction Company Ltd** dated: **29th December 1980**

[1] ~~and to which notice of the Engineer's decision has not been received.~~

is hereby
IN CONSEQUENCE OF WHICH notice ~~was~~ given in the [1] Employer [1] ~~Contractor~~ requiring the dispute(s) or difference(s) to be referred to arbitration ~~in letter(s)~~

~~from:~~ _____ dated: _____

[1] Delete as appropriate.

SD/4 Notice to concur

Part 2:   NOTICE TO CONCUR IN THE APPOINTMENT OF AN ARBITRATOR [2]

To: [1] Employer: __Wessex County Council__
~~[1] Contractor:~~
[1] Solicitor to Employer:
~~[1] Solicitor to Contractor:~~
Address: __County Council Offices__
  __Thomas Hardy Road__
  __Wiltonbury__
  __Wessex__

WE HEREBY GIVE NOTICE that we require the dispute(s) or difference(s) referred to in Part 1 of this Form to be referred to the arbitration of a person to be agreed upon between the Employer and the Contractor. We propose the following persons for your consideration and require your concurrence in and the appointment of one of them as Arbitrator within one calendar month of service of this Notice failing which we shall apply to the President of the Institution of Civil Engineers to appoint an Arbitrator.

Persons proposed as Arbitrator[3]:

Name: __A Fairman BSc FICE FCIArb__   Address: __The Manse   Penge__

or Name: __B Impartial MSc FICE FCIArb__   Address: __Rose Cottage   Blankville__

or Name: __C Twosides MA FICE FCIArb__   Address: __20 High Street   Anytown__

Dated this __Fourth__ day of __January__ 19__81__

Signature: __J Bloggs__   Director, The Universal Construction Company
       Company Ltd

~~[1] Employer~~ [1] Contractor ~~[1] Solicitor to Employer~~ ~~[1] Solicitor to Contractor~~

Address: __Construction House   Telford Road   Basingshot__
     __Hampshire__

---

[1] Delete as appropriate.
[2] In a Scottish arbitration the word 'Arbitrator' shall in accordance with section 2.2 of the Institution of Civil Engineers' Arbitration Procedure (1973) mean 'Arbiter'.
[3] The Institution publishes a *List of Arbitrators* which includes information on the arbitration experience and careers of the persons included. The List may be used by parties seeking to reach agreement on the choice of an arbitrator and is obtainable from the Arbitration Office at the Institution price £1.50. Cheques should be made payable to Thomas Telford Ltd.

SD/5 Application to the President

Part 3: APPLICATION TO THE PRESIDENT OF THE INSTITUTION OF CIVIL ENGINEERS TO APPOINT AN ARBITRATOR [2]

To the President   The Institution of Civil Engineers   Great George Street   London SW1P 3AA

IN THE MATTER OF THE DISPUTE(S) OR DIFFERENCE(S) referred to in Part 1 of this Form and since the parties have failed to agree upon an Arbitrator we hereby apply to you to appoint an Arbitrator.

We enclose a cheque[3] for ~~£20 plus~~ **£46 incl** VAT in respect of the charge made by the Institution of Civil Engineers towards administrative costs in connexion with this application.

The following is a brief description of the dispute(s) or difference(s)[4]:

Failure by the Engineer to certify payments in respect of:

(1) Additional costs incurred in dealing with unforeseeable ground conditions during construction of foundations;

(2) Additional costs resulting from delay and disruption of the construction programme caused by failure of the Engineer to issue drawings and instructions at a reasonable time.

Dated this **Eighth** day of **February** 19**81**

Signature: *J Bloggs*   Director, The Universal Construction Company Ltd

[1] ~~Employer~~ [1] Contractor [1] ~~Solicitor to Employer~~ [1] ~~Solicitor to Contractor~~

Address: Construction House   Telford Road
Basingshot   Hampshire

Part 4: APPOINTMENT OF AN ARBITRATOR BY THE PRESIDENT OF THE INSTITUTION OF CIVIL ENGINEERS

From the President:

To:

Copies for information to:

and:

I hereby appoint:

of:

Arbitrator in this matter

Dated this _____ day of _____ 19 ____

---

[1] Delete as appropriate.
[2] In a Scottish arbitration the word 'Arbitrator' shall in accordance with section 2.2 of the Institution of Civil Engineers' Arbitration Procedure (1973) mean 'Arbiter'.
[3] Cheques should be made payable to Thomas Telford Ltd.
[4] The description of the dispute(s) or difference(s) should be such as will enable the President to select an arbitrator experienced in the appropriate subject.

SD/6 Notice of arbitration and Notice to concur

From: The Speedybuild Construction Company Ltd
To: The Gigantic Property Company Ltd

15th March 1981

Dear Sirs

<u>Construction of Tower Block, Fred Needle Street</u>

We hereby give notice that a dispute has arisen from our contract with you for the construction of the above building, by reason of the failure of your Supervising Officer to certify certain payments, details of which were contained in our letter of 1st February 1980. We require such dispute to be referred to arbitration in accordance with Clause X of the said contract.

In accordance with that clause we submit the names of the following gentlemen and request that you concur in the appointment of one of them to be arbitrator in this reference:

Mr C Wren RIBA FCIArb of St Paul's Chambers London   or
Mr I Measure FRICS FCIArb of Yardstick Road Finchley   or
Mr Archibald Tect RIBA FCIArb of High Street Lowtown.

In the event that we do not receive a reply within 30 days of the date hereof, or that all of the above nominees are rejected without the substitution of another nominee acceptable to ourselves, we shall apply to the President of .... for the appointment of an arbitrator in accordance with the said Clause X of the contract.

Yours faithfully

for the Speedybuild Construction Company Ltd

P. O'Reilly
Director

SD/7 Application to the President to appoint an arbitrator

From: The Speedybuild Construction Company Ltd
To: The President, Institute of ....

20th April 1981

Dear Sir

Construction of Tower Block, Fred Needle Street

     We are under contract with the Gigantic Property Company Ltd to construct the above building, work on which is in our opinion practically completed. The contract provides for disputes to be determined by an arbitrator appointed, failing agreement, by the President of the Institute of ....

     Enclosed is a copy of our letter of 15th March 1981 addressed to our clients, the Employer in the contract, in which we sought agreement to the appointment of any one of the three nominees named therein. We have received no reply to this letter.

     Accordingly we request that you appoint an arbitrator to determine the matters in dispute. These matters concern the evaluation of additional work in deep excavations, including construction of a cofferdam, heavy reinforced concrete foundations and superstructure, and the evaluation of claims in respect of variations and of delays to the construction work. The sum in dispute is approximately £230 000 plus interest plus costs.

Yours faithfully

for the Speedybuild Construction Company Ltd

P. O'Reilly

P. O'Reilly
Director

SD/8 Notice of appointment

From: E Quitty BSc FICE FIStructE FCIArb
To: The Universal Construction Company Ltd
Wessex County Council

30th April 1981

Gentlemen

In the matter of the Arbitration Acts 1950-1979 and
In the matter of an arbitration between
The Universal Construction Company Ltd (CLAIMANTS) and
Wessex County Council (RESPONDENTS)

I am appointed (by the President of the Institution of......)*/(by agreement between the parties, such agreement being contained in letters dated 15 March and 27 March 1981 from the Claimants and from the Respondents, respectively)* to be arbitrator in the above reference. I hereby accept the appointment.

My charges will be at the rate of £.... per hour for time during which I engage myself upon, or which I allocate to, the duties of the reference, together with all expenses and outgoings incurred in the execution of those duties, including the cost of such legal advice as I may in my absolute discretion think it desirable to take. Provided that, if the arbitration shall proceed beyond 30th April 1982 the Claimants shall upon demand make interim payments on account of my fees and expenses. Provided further that if the arbitration shall proceed beyond April 1982 the rate in respect of my time shall be adjusted to allow for inflation.

I shall be pleased to receive your written acceptance of the above basis of my charges.

Yours faithfully

Edwin Quitty
Arbitrator

*Delete whichever is inapplicable

SD/9 Notice of appointment where parties are not represented

From: P R Obity MA FICE FCIArb
To: C L Aimant Esq
           R E Spondent Esq

31st May 1981

Gentlemen

Arbitration between C L Aimant and R E Spondent

I am appointed by the President of the Chartered Institute of Arbitrators to be Arbitrator in the above reference. I hereby accept the appointment.

In connection with the reference I have received the following documents, copies of which I understand to be in the possession of both parties:
(a) Copy of the contract dated 1st April 1980, from which the dispute arises.
(b) Copy of the application, dated 2nd April 1981, to the President of the Chartered Institute of Arbitrators for the appointment of an arbitrator, together with copies of documents referred to therein.

Before making arrangements for a Hearing and, if necessary, an inspection of the subject matter of the dispute, it is necessary to deal with certain preliminary matters to which I refer in the following paragraphs:

1. <u>Representation</u>

It is open to each party either to conduct his own case or to appoint a representative: for example a technical person or a lawyer. Each party must notify his intention in this matter to the other party in order that the other party may arrange similar representation if he wishes to do so.

In considering this point the parties should recognise that the cost of representation may be substantial, depending upon the type of representative chosen. In making my Award in due course it is part of my duty to award costs, and in doing so I shall have regard to the outcome of the claim and to the question whether or not costs were in my opinion incurred necessarily.

2. <u>Pleadings</u>

The law requires that each party shall be forewarned of the case to be presented by the other. This requirement is met by an exchange of Pleadings, which comprise Points of Claim, Points of Defence, and Points of Reply. Where there is a Counterclaim it is pleaded with the Points to Defence, and the Defence to the Counterclaim is pleaded with the Points of Reply. Each of these documents must set out in summary form the material facts upon which the party pleading intends to rely. It is open to either party, where necessary, to request Further and Better Particulars of the matters pleaded, and in doing so they must set out the precise particulars required.

The Claimant shall serve on the Respondent the Points of Claim not later than 14th June 1981, sending a copy of that document to me. Within 14 days of receipt of the Points of Claim the Respondent shall serve on the Claimant the Points of Defence (and Counterclaim if any) sending a copy to me. The Points of Reply (and Defence to Counterclaim if any) shall similarly be served, each within 14 days of receipt of the preceding pleading.

3. Discovery of Documents

All documents relating to the matters in dispute must be disclosed, whether or not they support the case of the party holding the documents. Within 7 days of the date of delivery of the last document in the Pleadings each party must prepare a list of all relevant documents that are or have been in their possession, and must send a copy of the list to the other party and to me. After exchange of the lists each party must within 7 days allow the other party to inspect the documents listed and must, where required, make copies of any of the documents, at the expense of the party requiring the copies.

All documents listed must be brought to the Hearing, and it is desirable that copies of all documents, or where this is impracticable, all important documents, should be made for my use and retention when making my Award.

4. Hearing

Subject to the completion of the above preliminaries in accordance with the programme defined in paragraphs 2 and 3 above it should be possible to arrange for the Hearing to take place in August 1981. I shall in due course notify the parties of the date, time and venue of the Hearing.

5. Other Matters

The parties are requested to acknowledge receipt of this letter and to state their intentions as regards representation, to which I refer in paragraph 1 above. The parties or their representatives should then proceed in accordance with paragraphs 2 and 3 above.

Should either party have difficulty in complying with the time limits defined herein they may apply to me for an extension, stating their reasons and the amount of extension required. I shall then determine the extension to be allowed, if any.

I shall not have any communication with a party without the knowledge of the other. For this reason I shall either address my letters to both parties or when writing to one party shall send a copy of my letter to the other. When writing to me the parties should send a copy of their letter to the other party, indicating on their letter to me that such copy has been sent.

For similar reasons I shall not have any communication with either party by telephone, except as may be necessary solely for the purpose of determining suitable dates for meetings or for the Hearing.

Yours faithfully

P R Obity
Arbitrator

SD/10 Notice of appointment where claim is small and parties are not represented

From: P R Obity MA FICE FCIArb
To: C L Aimant Esq
       R E Spondent Esq

31st May 1981

Gentlemen

<u>Arbitration between Claude Leslie Aimant and
Roger Ernest Spondent</u>

I am appointed by the President of the Chartered Institute of Arbitrators to be Arbitrator in the above reference. I hereby accept the appointment.

In connection with the reference I have received the following documents, copies of which I understand to be in the possession of both parties:
(a) The contract from which the dispute arises, namely a contract between the parties dated 10th April 1980;
(b) An application by the Claimant, dated 2nd May 1981, to the President of the Chartered Institute of Arbitrators for the appointment of an arbitrator, together with copies of documents referred to therein.

I note that neither party is represented by a legal or a technical person, and I wish to make it clear that each party is free to arrange such representation if they so wish, provided that the party makes its intentions known to the other party and to me. In reaching a decision on this point the parties should recognise that such representation may incur substantial cost. It is part of my duty, in due course, to award costs at my discretion, and in exercising that discretion I shall have regard to the outcome of the arbitration and to the question whether or not in my opinion costs were incurred necessarily.

Having regard to the small sum in dispute in this reference the parties may wish to adopt, by agreement, the following procedure which is suggested as a means of minimising costs:

1. That neither party be represented by a lawyer or by an expert.
2. That the matters in dispute be determined upon written evidence only presented by the parties, together with an inspection, if necessary, of the subject matter of the dispute in the presence of both parties.
3. That the programme shall be:
   (a) Within 14 days of the date by which both parties have agreed to adopt this procedure the Claimant shall submit to me and to the Respondent a Statement of his Claim, together with documentary evidence in support of that Claim and any other submission he may wish to make.
   (b) Within 14 days of receipt of the above the Respondent shall submit to me and to the Claimant a Statement of his Defence, together with documentary evidence in support of that Defence, and any other submission he may wish to make.
   (c) Within 14 days thereafter the Claimant may if he wishes submit to me and to the Respondent a Reply to any allegation in the Defence, where such allegation has not been dealt with in the Claim.
   (d) Thereafter on a date to be arranged I will inspect the subject matter of the claim in the presence of both parties, who will be permitted to draw to my attention any matters they may wish me to note but not to make any further representation.

I request that both parties advise me and each other whether or not they agree to adopt the procedure detailed in paragraphs numbered 1, 2 and 3 above, and if both parties do so agree, that the Claimant proceed in accordance with item 3(a). If either party, or both parties, do not so agree, then it will become necessary to adopt more elaborate procedures which will of course involve greater costs. If necessary I shall give instructions as to such procedures.

Yours faithfully

P.R. Obity

P R Obity
Arbitrator

SD/11 Check list for preliminary meeting

Meeting date............ time......... place......................

Parties: Claimants   Respondents

    Name   ....

    Represented by   ....

    Position   ....

    Firm   ....

Date and Form of Contract .... Edition....... Signed.........

Arbitration clause therein...........   Validity checked......

Subject matter of dispute..

Amount of Claim (approx).......................

Subject matter of Counterclaim if any..

Amount of Counterclaim (approx)...............

(Check validity of appointment:

Valid arbitration agreement?......   Valid appointment procedure?......

Subject matter within competence?......   No prior knowledge?..........

No interest in either party?........   Relationship to be disclosed?.....)

                          Claimants   Respondents

Counsel to be briefed?   .... Fit?.....

Experts to be appointed?   ....

Evidence on affidavit?   ....

Agreement to transcript?   ....

Pleadings: timing: Points of Claim   ....

                   Points of Defence (and Counterclaim)   ....

                   Points of Reply (and Defence to CC)   ....

                   Reply to Defence to Counterclaim   ....

                   Close of Pleadings 7 days later?   ....

Discovery of Documents: Exchange lists within (days) ....

                       Inspection by   ....

Provisional date for Hearing............... Estimated duration..........

Venue for Hearing................. To be booked by........................

Reasons to be given in Award?...................

Exclusion agreement to be made?.................

Inspection of subject matter?................... Date............

Standard Instructions:
    Figures to be agreed as figures where possible.
    Photographs, plans and documents to be agreed where possible.
    There shall be liberty to apply.
    Parties when writing to me shall send a copy of their letter and any enclosures to the other party, indicating that they have done so.
    There shall be no communication between the parties and myself by telephone, except for the purpose of fixing meeting dates.
    Costs of this application and Order to be costs of the reference.

SD/12   Order for directions

In the matter of the Arbitration Acts 1950-1979 and
In the matter of an arbitration between

        The Universal Construction Company Ltd   **CLAIMANTS**
        and
        Wessex County Council   **RESPONDENTS**

ORDER FOR DIRECTIONS

By consent/
Upon hearing the parties' representatives on both sides the following Directions are given and I hereby Order as follows:

1. That there shall be Pleadings in this arbitration as follows:
   Points of Claim to be delivered within .28. days of the date hereof. Points of Defence (and Counterclaim if any) to be delivered within ..28... days thereafter. Points of Reply (and Defence to Counterclaim if any) to be delivered within .14. days thereafter. Points of Reply to Defence to Counterclaim, if any, to be delivered within .14. days thereafter. Pleadings shall be deemed to be closed 7 days thereafter.

2. That there shall be Discovery of Documents as follows:
   Within .14. days of the close of Pleadings the Claimants and the Respondents shall each deliver to the other a List of Documents which are or have been in their possession or power relating to the matters in question in this arbitration and inspection shall be given within ...7... days therafter.

3. That figures be agreed as figures where possible, and that correspondence, photographs and plans be agreed where possible.

4. That a copy of any communication sent to me by either party shall be sent simultaneously to the other party, the original being marked to indicate such copy has been sent.

5. That the Hearing of this arbitration be provisionally arranged to commence at 10.30 a.m. on Monday 14th September 1981, and be estimated to last 4 days. The Hearing to take place at Bank Chambers High Street Wiltonbury.

6. That experts be limited to ..2.. on each side.

7. That by consent the Claimants shall arrange for a transcript of the Hearing to be taken and one copy of such transcript (or such part of it as I may require) to be prepared for my use. The costs thereof to be costs in the arbitration.

8. That I shall view the subject matter of the arbitration at 11..00 a.m. on .21st. September 1981 in the presence of representatives of both parties.

9. That there shall be liberty to apply.

10. That the costs of this application and Order shall be costs in the arbitration.

Fit for Counsel.

Dated this .26th. day of May 1981

E Quitty
Arbitrator

To: Claimants' solicitors
Respondents' solicitors

SD/13   Points of Claim

In the matter of the Arbitration Acts 1950-1979 and
In the matter of an arbitration between

       The Universal Construction Company Ltd   <u>CLAIMANTS</u>
       and
       Wessex County Council   <u>RESPONDENTS</u>

P O I N T S   O F   C L A I M

1. The Claimants are Civil Engineering Contractors based at Basingshot Hampshire. The Respondents are a County Council acting as agents for the Department of Transport.
2. By a contract in writing dated the second day of January 1979 the Claimants undertook to construct, complete and maintain certain works of civil engineering construction, namely a Bridge over the river Avon, being Contract No 6 of the M100 Motorway, in consideration for which the Respondents undertook to pay to the Claimants the contract Price at the times and in the manner prescribed in the Contract.
3. The said Contract incorporates a document commonly known as the ICE Conditions of Contract: Fifth Edition (June 1973)(Revised January 1979) wherein it is provided:
    (a) Under Clause 12 that the Contractor shall subject to certain conditions be paid the reasonable cost of carrying out additional works and the reasonable costs incurred by reason of unavoidable delay or disruption suffered as a result of encountering physical conditions or artificial obstructions such as could not be reasonably have been foreseen by an experienced contractor.
    (b) Under Clause 7 (3) that the Contractor shall subject to certain provisions be paid the amount of such cost as may be incurred by reason of any failure or inability of the Engineer to issue at a time reasonable in all the circumstances drawings or instructions requested by the contractor and considered necessary by the Engineer.
4. In breach of the said Clauses 12 and 7 (3) of the contract the Engineer failed to certify payment of certain sums to which the Claimants are entitled and in consequence the Claimants have suffered loss and damage.

PARTICULARS

Under Clause 12:

Hire of additional plant	16 000
Additional labour costs	12 000
Site oncosts (3 weeks)	4 200
	£32 200
Plus Head Office oncosts at 8%	2 576
Total under Clause 12	£34 776

Under Clause 7 (3):

Hire of plant for 5 weeks	29 400
Labour costs for 5 weeks	20 000
Site oncosts for 5 weeks	7 000
	£56 400
Plus Head Office oncosts at 8%	4 512
Total under Clause 7 (3)	£60 912

5. And accordingly the Claimants claim £95 688 plus interest thereon.

BARRY STER

SERVED this 19th Day of June 1981 by Smith, Jones & Company of 98 Smeaton Road Basingshot Hampshire, Solicitors for the Claimants.

To: Respondents
    Arbitrator

SD/14   Points of Defence

In the matter of the Arbitration Acts 1950-1979 and
In the matter of an arbitration between

        The Universal Construction Company Ltd   CLAIMANTS
        and
        Wessex County Council   RESPONDENTS

POINTS OF DEFENCE

1. Save that the Contract incorporates, in addition to the ICE Conditions of Contract, a Specification and Contract drawings numbered 1 to 26, paragraphs 1, 2 and 3 of the Points of Claim are admitted. It is admitted and averred that the Contract is subject to the ICE Conditions of Contract (Fifth Edition) to which the Respondents will refer as may be necessary for their full content.
2. Paragraphs 4 and 5 of the Points of Claim are denied.
3. Save as is herein expressly admitted the Repondents deny each and every allegation contained in the Points of Claim as if the same were set out and specifically denied seriatim.
4. Further or in the alternative if which is not admitted the Claimants incurred additional costs of plant labour and/or oncosts such costs resulted from failure by the Claimants to make adequate provision for ground conditions which were foreseeable by an experienced contractor and/or from failure by the Claimants to provide suitable plant for execution of the contract works.

                                              PETER COUNSEL

SERVED this 17th Day of July 1981 by Black, White & Company of 22 Plastic Buildings Upper Temple London, Solicitors for the Respondents.

To: Claimants
       Arbitrator

SD/15   Points of Reply

In the matter of the Arbitration Acts 1950-1979 and
In the matter of an arbitration between

    The Universal Construction Company Ltd CLAIMANTS
    and
    Wessex County Council RESPONDENTS

P O I N T S   O F   R E P L Y

1. Save insofar as the Points of Defence consists of admissions the Claimants join issue with the Respondents in each and every allegation contained therein.
2. It is denied that the Claimants failed to make adequate provision for ground conditions or that such conditions were foreseeable by an experienced contractor as alleged in paragraph 4 of the Points of Defence.
3. It is denied that the Claimants failed to provide suitable plant for the execution of the contract works as further alleged in paragraph 4 of the Points of Defence.

        BARRY STER

SERVED this 30th Day of July by Smith, Jones & Company of 98 Smeaton Road Basingshot Hampshire, Solicitors for the Claimants.

To: Respondents
   Arbitrator

SD/16   Request for further and better particulars

<u>In</u> the matter of the Arbitration Acts 1950-1979 and
<u>In</u> the matter of an arbitration between

        The Universal Construction Company Ltd   <u>CLAIMANTS</u>
        and
        Wessex County Council   <u>RESPONDENTS</u>

REQUEST FOR FURTHER AND BETTER PARTICULARS OF THE POINTS OF CLAIM

<u>Under Paragraph 4</u>

(a) Set out with full particularity each and every item of additional plant alleged to have been hired, stating the dates of commencement and of termination of the alleged hire, the purpose for which the item is alleged to have been used, hire charges per hour or per day and all further details if any needed to show how the sums claimed are made up.

(b) Set out with full particularity the name and trade of each and every additional man alleged to have been employed, the dates of commencement and completion of such employment, the type of work upon which engaged, the hourly wage rate alleged to have been paid together with details of all such additional payments, allowances and employment expenses as are alleged to have been incurred, to show how the sums claimed in respect of Labour costs are made up.

(c) Set out with full particularity details of all costs alleged to have been incurred under the heading 'Site Oncosts' stating the exact period or periods during which such costs were alleged to have been incurred and the rate of such costs per day or per week as may be applicable to each of the items claimed.

                                        PETER COUNSEL

SERVED this 17th Day of July 1981 by Black, White & Company of 22 Plastic Buildings Upper Temple London, Solicitors for the Respondents.

To: Claimants
       Arbitrator

SD/17 Further and better particulars

In the matter of the Arbitration Acts 1950-1979 and
In the matter of an arbitration between

        The Universal Construction Company Ltd   CLAIMANTS
        and
        Wessex County Council   RESPONDENTS

FURTHER AND BETTER PARTICULARS OF THE POINTS OF CLAIM

Under Paragraph 4

(a)
Item of Plant	Date of Hire From	To	Used for	Hire charge per hour	Total Cost £
Hymac 880	21.9	15.12	Trench excavation	26.10	12 528
Crane 50 t	21.9	15.12	Piling		

                                    etc etc

To: Respondents
      Arbitrator

SD/18 Scott Schedule

ITEM No	CLAIM	AMOUNT	DEFENCE	OFFER	ARBITRATOR'S FINDING	AWARD
1	Extension of time: inclement weather	6 weeks	Part of lost time foreseeable	2 weeks		
2	Extension of time: drwgs issued late	8 weeks	No delay caused	Nil		
3	Payment for ditto	£4 000	No liability	Nil		
4	Variations: founds: additional time	8 weeks	Admitted	8 weeks		
5	Ditto: additional excavation	£6 000	Quantity agreed. Rate reduced	£4 500		
6	Ditto: alterations to sheet piling	£9 500	Piling to increased depth should have been allowed for	Nil		
7	Variations: general delay & disruption	20 weeks	Denied	Nil		
8	Ditto: additional labour costs	£8 700	Denied	Nil		
9	Ditto: additional site oncosts	£3 600	Denied	Nil		

SD/19   List of documents

In the matter of the Arbitration Acts 1950-1979 and
In the matter of an arbitration between

        The Universal Construction Company Ltd   CLAIMANTS
        and
        Wessex County Council   RESPONDENTS

LIST OF DOCUMENTS

The following is a list of the documents relating to the matters in question in this arbitration which are or have been in the possession, custody or power of the Claimants.

1. The Claimants have in their possession all of those documents in the First Schedule hereto that are marked 'From R' and 'From E'.
2. The Claimants have had but do not now have in their possession, custody or power all of those documents in the First Schedule hereto that are marked 'From C'.
3. The Claimants object to the production of the documents in the Second Schedule hereto on the ground that the said documents are privileged.
4. Of the documents in the said First Schedule hereto those marked 'From C' were last in the Claimants' possession custody or power on the dates thereof.
5. Neither the Claimants nor their Solicitors nor any other person on their behalf has now or ever has had in their possession custody or power any document of any description relating to the matters in question in this arbitration, other than the documents listed in the First and Second Schedules hereto.

SERVED this 20th Day of August 1981 by Smith, Jones & Co of 98 Smeaton Road Basingshot Hampshire, Solicitors for the Claimants.

FIRST SCHEDULE

C = Claimants
E = Engineer
R = Respondents

Document No	Date	From	To	Remarks
1	25.09.78	R	C	Letter inviting C to tender and enclosing tender drawings and documents all as enumerated therein
2	27.09.78	C	R	Acknowledged receipt of 1. Will tender.
3	15.11.78	C	R	Enclosed tender.
4	25.11.78	R	C	Tender being considered. Meeting to discuss at CC Offices 02.12.78
5	26.11.78	C	R	Acknowledged 4. Will attend meeting.

6	15.12.78	R	C	Tender accepted. Enclose Forms of Agreement and Bond. Insurance details to be submitted.
7	21.12.78	C	R	Enclosed executed contract documents etc.
8	05.01.79	R	C	Acknowledged 7. Contract executed 2 Jan. Engineer will send drawings.
9	10.01.79	E	C	Enclosed 2 sets of working drawings and documents. Site meeting 18.01.79. Start date 01.02.79. Programme required.
10	20.01.79	C	E	Enclosed programme & notes on site meeting. Method statement.
11				

etc etc

SD/20 Proof of evidence

WILLIAM SMITH, of 23 Lowtown Cottages, Basingshot, Hampshire, a chartered engineer, will say:

I have been employed by the Universal Construction Company Ltd as a civil engineer since 1970. I first joined the company as a site engineer, and was promoted to senior engineer in 1975 and to site agent on 1st December 1978, when I was appointed to take charge of the River Avon Bridge contract. I am still employed by the company as a site agent.

Excavation for the east abutment of the bridge was commenced on 5th March 1979, using trench sheets 3.5 metres long to support the sides, because boreholes indicated that the hard sandstone on which the abutment was to be founded would be encountered at a depth of about 2.5 metres. Upon reaching this depth however the ground was found to be soft silty clay. I arranged for a hole to be made using a hand auger, and this showed that the sandstone would not be encountered until a depth below original ground level of 4.0 metres was reached.

I asked the Resident Engineer Mr. Cleverdick to issue a variation order to cover extraction of the trench sheets and replacement by steel sheet piles 5.5 metres in length, but this he refused to do because he said that was my worry. Eventually after some considerable delay while I arranged for the Chief Engineer of my company to visit the site I sent to the Resident Engineer a notice (document 26, bundle C) under clause 12 of the conditions of contract and arranged for extraction of the trench sheets and for driving of the steel sheet piles I had proposed. It was not however possible to proceed with this work immediately because I was unable to obtain the necessary piles for $2\frac{1}{2}$ weeks, during which period the crane which was required for piling and for excavation was standing, there being no other work for it on site. I also had to obtain a piling hammer suitable for driving Larssen 1B piles, and this caused a further delay of 1 week.

SD/21   Award

In the matter of the Arbitration Acts 1950-1979 and
In the matter of an arbitration between

        The Universal Construction Company Ltd   CLAIMANTS
        and
        Wessex County Council   RESPONDENTS

AWARD

WHEREAS:

1. By a Contract in writing dated the Second Day of January 1979 the Claimants undertook to construct, complete and maintain certain works of civil engineering construction namely Motorway M100: Contract No 6: Bridge over River Avon, in consideration for which the Respondents undertook to pay to the Claimants the Contract Price at the times and in the manner prescribed in the Contract.

2. The said Contract provided that any dispute between the parties that might arise from it should be referred to the arbitration of a person to be agreed upon between the parties, or failing agreement to be appointed upon the application of either party by the President of the Institution of Civil Engineers.

3. A dispute having arisen and following an application by the Claimants on the Eighth Day of February 1981 the President of the said Institution did appoint me, Edwin Quitty, to be Arbitrator in the reference, which appointment I accepted by notice in writing to both parties on the Thirtieth Day of April 1981.

4. A preliminary meeting for Directions was convened by me and was held in Wiltonbury on the Twenty-fifth Day of May 1981.

5. An Order for Directions was issued by me on the Twenty-sixth Day of May 1981.

6. After an exchange of Pleadings and Discovery of Documents in accordance with the said Order a Hearing was held in Wiltonbury on the Twenty-fifth Day of September 1981.

NOW I THE SAID EDWIN QUITTY having heard and considered the evidence both oral and written adduced by both parties and the addresses to me made by Counsel on their behalf DO HEREBY MAKE AND PUBLISH THIS MY AWARD.

I FIND THAT:

1. The Claimants were required under a contract with the Respondents to construct a bridge to carry the M100 Motorway over the River Avon.
2. During the construction of the east abutment of that bridge subsoil conditions were encountered which prevented that abutment from being founded at the level that had been indicated on the drawings, because at that level the ground was too soft.
3. The Engineer ordered the Claimants to excavate to a greater depth than had been allowed for in the said contract, and this required for its safe execution that the Claimants should obtain special plant and equipment for the work.

4. The Engineer failed to certify payment of certain sums to which the Claimants are entitled under Clause 12 of the Contract: such sums being the amount of costs reasonably incurred by the Claimants in carrying out the additional works made necessary by the unforeseen ground conditions.
5. During the course of the works the Engineer issued certain additional drawings and instructions necessary for the execution of those works.
6. Such drawings and instructions were in certain cases issued immediately before the dates indicated on the Claimants' construction programme, which had been agreed to be the Engineer, as the dates of commencement of the items of work referred to in the drawings and instructions, but not in sufficient time to allow the Claimants to plan the execution of those works, to design necessary temporary works and to obtain items of special plant and equipment that were needed for its execution.
7. In consequence of the above the construction works were delayed, and additional costs were incurred by the Claimants in respect of such delays.
8. The Engineer failed to certify payment of certain sums to which the Claimants are entitled under Clause 7(3) of the Contract in respect of the matters referred to in paragraphs 5, 6 and 7 above.
9. Prior to the Hearing the parties did agree certain figures, as figures, representing the additional costs incurred by the Claimants in respect of additional works at the east abutment, in the sum of Twenty-seven thousand five hundred pounds (£27 500) and in respect of a delay of eight weeks in the sum of Fifty-five thousand pounds (£55 000).

I HOLD THAT:

The Respondents are liable to the Claimants in Breach of Contract for the additional costs referred to in Paragraphs 4 and 8 of my Findings, the amount of such costs being the sums referred to in Paragraph 9 of my Findings, plus interest, plus costs.

AND ACCORDINGLY I HEREBY AWARD AND DIRECT THAT:

1. The Respondents shall within 28 days of the date on which this Award is taken up by either party pay to the Claimants the sum of One hundred and eleven thousand three hundred and seventy-five pounds (£111 375) including Twenty-eight thousand eight hundred and seventy-five pounds (£28 875) in respect of interest, in full and final settlement of all claims referred to me herein.
2. The Respondents shall pay the Claimants' costs of the reference, such costs if not agreed to be taxed upon a party and party basis.
3. The Respondents shall pay and bear the costs of this my Award which I hereby tax and settle in the sum of Twelve hundred and sixty pounds (£1 260) plus Value Added Tax of One hundred and eighty-nine pounds (£189), provided that if such costs have already been paid by the Claimants the Respondents shall within 28 days of the date on which this Award is taken up by either party reimburse the Claimants accordingly.

FIT FOR COUNSEL

Given under my hand this Thirtieth Day of September 1981

Edwin Quitty
Arbitrator

In the presence of:
Witness: P Polly
Address: The Aviary Birdcage Walk Wiltonbury
Occupation: Secretary

SD/22 Notice of publication of award

From: E Quitty BSc FICE FIStructE FCIArb
To: The Universal Construction Company Ltd
          The Chief Executive, Wessex County Council

30th September 1981

Gentlemen

          Arbitration between the Universal Construction Company Ltd

                                         - and -

                             Wessex County Council

          I have today made and published my Award in the above reference, and it is available for collection or dispatch to either party upon payment of my charges in the sum of £1 260 plus £189 VAT, making a total of £1 449.

          The Award includes provision for reimbursement of these charges by the party responsible for them in the event that the other party takes up the Award.

Yours faithfully

Edwin Quitty
Arbitrator

Arbitration Act, 1950
14 Geo. 6. Ch. 27

(Showing amendments and deletions as a result of the Arbitration Act 1975 and the Arbitration Act 1979)

ARRANGEMENT OF SECTIONS
Part I
General Provisions as to Arbitration

Effect of Arbitration Agreements, &c.

Section
1. Authority of arbitrators and umpires to be irrevocable.
2. Death of party.
3. Bankruptcy.
4. Staying court proceedings where there is submission to arbitration.
5. Reference of interpleader issues to arbitration.

Arbitrators and Umpires
6. When reference is to a single arbitrator.
7. Power of parties in certain cases to supply vacancy.
8. Umpires.
9. Agreements for reference to three arbitrators.
10. Power of court in certain cases to appoint an arbitrator or umpire.
11. Reference to official referee.

Conduct of Proceedings, Witnesses, &c
12. Conduct of proceedings, witnesses, &c.

Provisions as to Awards
13. Time for making award.
14. Interim awards.
15. Specific performance.
16. Awards to be final.
17. Power to correct slips.

Costs, Fees and Interest
18. Costs.
19. Taxation of arbitrator's or umpire's fees.
20. Interest on awards.

~~Special Cases~~, Remission and Setting aside of Awards, &c. REPEALED
21. ~~Statement of case.~~
22. Power to remit award.

Section
23. Removal of arbitrator and setting aside of award.
24. Power of court to give relief where arbitrator is not impartial or the dispute involves question of fraud.
25. Power of court where arbitrator is removed or authority of arbitrator is revoked.

Enforcement of Award

26. Enforcement of award.

Miscellaneous

27. Power of court to extend time for commencing arbitration proceedings.
28. Terms as to costs, &c.
29. Extension of s. 496 of the Merchant Shipping Act, 1894.
30. Crown to be bound.
31. Application of Part I to statutory arbitrations.
32. Meaning of " arbitration agreement ".
33. Operation of Part I.
34. Extent of Part I.

Part II
Enforcement of certain Foreign Awards

35. Awards to which Part II applies.
36. Effect of foreign awards.
37. Conditions for enforcement of foreign awards.
38. Evidence.
39. Meaning of " final award ".
40. Saving for other rights, &c.
41. Application of Part II to Scotland.
42. Application of Part II to Northern Ireland.
43. Saving for pending proceedings.

Part III
General

44. Short title, commencement and repeal.

Schedules.

First Schedule.—Protocol on Arbitration Clauses signed on behalf of His Majesty at a Meeting of the Assembly of the League of Nations held on the twenty-fourth day of September, nineteen hundred and twenty-three.

Second Schedule.—Convention on the Execution of Foreign Arbitral Awards signed at Geneva on behalf of His Majesty on the twenty-sixth day of September, nineteen hundred and twenty-seven.

CHAPTER 27

An Act to consolidate the Arbitration Acts, 1889 to 1934.
[28th July 1950.]

BE it enacted by the King's most Excellent Majesty, by and with the advice and consent of the Lords Spiritual and Temporal, and Commons, in this present Parliament assembled, and by the authority of the same, as follows:—

Part I

General Provisions as to Arbitration

Effect of Arbitration Agreements, &c.

1. The authority of an arbitrator or umpire appointed by or by virtue of an arbitration agreement shall, unless a contrary intention is expressed in the agreement, be irrevocable except by leave of the High Court or a judge thereof. *Authority of arbitrators and umpires to be irrevocable.*

2.—(1) An arbitration agreement shall not be discharged by the death of any party thereto, either as respects the deceased or any other party, but shall in such an event be enforceable by or against the personal representative of the deceased. *Death of party.*

(2) The authority of an arbitrator shall not be revoked by the death of any party by whom he was appointed.

(3) Nothing in this section shall be taken to affect the operation of any enactment or rule of law by virtue of which any right of action is extinguished by the death of a person.

3.—(1) Where it is provided by a term in a contract to which a bankrupt is a party that any differences arising thereout or in connection therewith shall be referred to arbitration, the said term shall, if the trustee in bankruptcy adopts the contract, be enforceable by or against him so far as relates to any such differences. *Bankruptcy*

110   ARBITRATION ACT 1950

PART I
—cont.

(2) Where a person who has been adjudged bankrupt had, before the commencement of the bankruptcy, become a party to an arbitration agreement, and any matter to which the agreement applies requires to be determined in connection with or for the purposes of the bankruptcy proceedings, then, if the case is one to which subsection (1) of this section does not apply, any other party to the agreement or, with the consent of the committee of inspection, the trustee in bankruptcy, may apply to the court having jurisdiction in the bankruptcy proceedings for an order directing that the matter in question shall be referred to arbitration in accordance with the agreement, and that court may, if it is of opinion that, having regard to all the circumstances of the case, the matter ought to be determined by arbitration, make an order accordingly.

Staying court proceedings where there is submission to arbitration.

4.—(1) If any party to an arbitration agreement, or any person claiming through or under him, commences any legal proceedings in any court against any other party to the agreement, or any person claiming through or under him, in respect of any matter agreed to be referred, any party to those legal proceedings may at any time after appearance, and before delivering any pleadings or taking any other steps in the proceedings, apply to that court to stay the proceedings, and that court or a judge thereof, if satisfied that there is no sufficient reason why the matter should not be referred in accordance with the agreement, and that the applicant was, at the time when the proceedings were commenced, and still remains, ready and willing to do all things necessary to the proper conduct of the arbitration, may make an order staying the proceedings.

REPEALED

(2) Notwithstanding anything in this Part of this Act, if any party to a submission to arbitration made in pursuance of an agreement to which the protocol set out in the First Schedule to this Act applies, or any person claiming through or under him, commences any legal proceedings in any court against any other party to the submission, or any person claiming through or under him, in respect of any matter agreed to be referred, any party to those legal proceedings may at any time after appearance, and before delivering any pleadings or taking any other steps in the proceedings, apply to that court to stay the proceedings, and that court or a judge thereof, unless satisfied that the agreement or arbitration has become inoperative or cannot proceed or that there is not in fact any dispute between the parties with regard to the matter agreed to be referred, shall make an order staying the proceedings.

Reference of interpleader issues to arbitration.

5. Where relief by way of interpleader is granted and it appears to the High Court that the claims in question are matters to which an arbitration agreement, to which the claimants are parties, applies, the High Court may direct the issue between the claimants to be determined in accordance with the agreement.

Arbitrators and Umpires

PART I
—*cont.*

6. Unless a contrary intention is expressed therein, every arbitration agreement shall, if no other mode of reference is provided, be deemed to include a provision that the reference shall be to a single arbitrator.

When reference is to a single arbitrator.

7. Where an arbitration agreement provides that the reference shall be to two arbitrators, one to be appointed by each party, then, unless a contrary intention is expressed therein—

Power of parties in certain cases to supply vacancy.

  (a) if either of the appointed arbitrators refuses to act, or is incapable of acting, or dies, the party who appointed him may appoint a new arbitrator in his place ;

  (b) if, on such a reference, one party fails to appoint an arbitrator, either originally, or by way of substitution as aforesaid, for seven clear days after the other party, having appointed his arbitrator, has served the party making default with notice to make the appointment, the party who has appointed an arbitrator may appoint that arbitrator to act as sole arbitrator in the reference and his award shall be binding on both parties as if he had been appointed by consent :

Provided that the High Court or a judge thereof may set aside any appointment made in pursuance of this section.

8.—(1) Unless a contrary intention is expressed therein, every arbitration agreement shall, where the reference is to two arbitrators, be deemed to include a provision that the two arbitrators* ~~shall appoint an umpire immediately~~ after they are themselves appointed.**

Umpires.

*may appoint an umpire at any time

**and shall do so forthwith if they cannot agree.

(2) Unless a contrary intention is expressed therein, every arbitration agreement shall, where such a provision is applicable to the reference, be deemed to include a provision that if the arbitrators have delivered to any party to the arbitration agreement, or to the umpire, a notice in writing stating that they cannot agree, the umpire may forthwith enter on the reference in lieu of the arbitrators.

(3) At any time after the appointment of an umpire, however appointed, the High Court may, on the application of any party to the reference and notwithstanding anything to the contrary in the arbitration agreement, order that the umpire shall enter upon the reference in lieu of the arbitrators and as if he were a sole arbitrator.

9.—~~(1) Where an arbitration agreement provides that the~~ reference shall be to three arbitrators, one to be ~~appointed by~~ each party and the third to be ~~appointed by~~ the two appointed by the parties, ~~the agreement~~ shall have effect as if it provided ~~for the appointment of an umpire, and not for the appointment~~

~~Agreements~~ for reference to three arbitrators.
SEE 1979 ACT 6

PART I
—cont.

~~of a third arbitrator, by the two arbitrators appointed by the~~ parties.

(2) Where an arbitration agreement provides that the reference shall be to three arbitrators to be appointed otherwise than as mentioned in subsection (1) of this section, the award of any two ~~of the arbitrators shall be binding~~.

Power of court in certain cases to appoint an arbitrator or umpire.

10. In any of the following cases—

(a) where an arbitration agreement provides that the reference shall be to a single arbitrator, and all the parties do not, after differences have arisen, concur in the appointment of an arbitrator;

(b) if an appointed arbitrator refuses to act, or is incapable of acting, or dies, and the arbitration agreement does not show that it was intended that the vacancy should not be supplied and the parties do not supply the vacancy;

*required or are

(c) where the parties or two arbitrators are* at liberty to appoint an umpire or third arbitrator and do not appoint him, ~~or where two arbitrators are required to appoint an umpire and do not appoint him~~;

(d) where an appointed umpire or third arbitrator refuses to act, or is incapable of acting, or dies, and the arbitration agreement does not show that it was intended that the vacancy should not be supplied, and the parties or arbitrators do not supply the vacancy;

any party may serve the other parties or the arbitrators, as the case may be, with a written notice to appoint or, as the case may be, concur in appointing, an arbitrator, umpire or third arbitrator, and if the appointment is not made within seven clear days after the service of the notice, the High Court or a judge thereof may, on application by the party who gave the notice, appoint an arbitrator, umpire or third arbitrator who shall have the like powers to act in the reference and make an award as if he had been appointed by consent of all parties.

**SEE 1979 ACT 6 (4)

Reference to official referee.

**11. Where an arbitration agreement provides that the reference shall be to an official referee, any official referee to whom application is made shall, subject to any order of the High Court or a judge thereof as to transfer or otherwise, hear and determine the matters agreed to be referred.

Conduct of Proceedings, Witnesses, &c.

Conduct of proceedings, witnesses, &c.

12.—(1) Unless a contrary intention is expressed therein, every arbitration agreement shall, where such a provision is applicable to the reference, be deemed to contain a provision that the parties to the reference, and all persons claiming through them respectively, shall, subject to any legal objection, submit to be examined by the arbitrator or umpire, on oath or affirmation, in relation to the matters in dispute, and shall, subject as aforesaid, produce before the arbitrator or umpire all documents within their possession or power respectively which may be required or called for, and do all other things which during the proceedings on the reference the arbitrator or umpire may require.

(2) Unless a contrary intention is expressed therein, every arbitration agreement shall, where such a provision is applicable to the reference, be deemed to contain a provision that the witnesses on the reference shall, if the arbitrator or umpire thinks fit, be examined on oath or affirmation.

(3) An arbitrator or umpire shall, unless a contrary intention is expressed in the arbitration agreement, have power to administer oaths to, or take the affirmations of, the parties to and witnesses on a reference under the agreement.

(4) Any party to a reference under an arbitration agreement may sue out a writ of subpoena ad testificandum or a writ of subpoena duces tecum, but no person shall be compelled under any such writ to produce any document which he could not be compelled to produce on the trial of an action, and the High Court or a judge thereof may order that a writ of subpoena ad testificandum or of subpoena duces tecum shall issue to compel the attendance before an arbitrator or umpire of a witness wherever he may be within the United Kingdom.

(5) The High Court or a judge thereof may also order that a writ of habeas corpus ad testificandum shall issue to bring up a prisoner for examination before an arbitrator or umpire.

(6) The High Court shall have, for the purpose of and in relation to a reference, the same power of making orders in respect of—
- (a) security for costs;
- (b) discovery of documents and interrogatories;
- (c) the giving of evidence by affidavit;
- (d) examination on oath of any witness before an officer of the High Court or any other person, and the issue of a commission or request for the examination of a witness out of the jurisdiction;
- (e) the preservation, interim custody or sale of any goods which are the subject matter of the reference;
- (f) securing the amount in dispute in the reference;
- (g) the detention, preservation or inspection of any property or thing which is the subject of the reference or as to which any question may arise therein, and authorising for any of the purposes aforesaid any persons to enter

PART I
—cont.

PART I
—cont.

upon or into any land or building in the possession of any party to the reference, or authorising any samples to be taken or any observation to be made or experiment to be tried which may be necessary or expedient for the purpose of obtaining full information or evidence ; and

(*h*) interim injunctions or the appointment of a receiver ;

as it has for the purpose of and in relation to an action or matter in the High Court:

Provided that nothing in this subsection shall be taken to prejudice any power which may be vested in an arbitrator or umpire of making orders with respect to any of the matters aforesaid.

Provisions as to Awards

Time for making award.
13.—(1) Subject to the provisions of subsection (2) of section twenty-two of this Act, and anything to the contrary in the arbitration agreement, an arbitrator or umpire shall have power to make an award at any time.

(2) The time, if any, limited for making an award, whether under this Act or otherwise, may from time to time be enlarged by order of the High Court or a judge thereof, whether that time has expired or not.

(3) The High Court may, on the application of any party to a reference, remove an arbitrator or umpire who fails to use all reasonable dispatch in entering on and proceeding with the reference and making an award, and an arbitrator or umpire who is removed by the High Court under this subsection shall not be entitled to receive any remuneration in respect of his services.

For the purposes of this subsection, the expression " proceeding with a reference " includes, in a case where two arbitrators are unable to agree, giving notice of that fact to the parties and to the umpire.

Interim awards.
14. Unless a contrary intention is expressed therein, every arbitration agreement shall, where such a provision is applicable to the reference, be deemed to contain a provision that the arbitrator or umpire may, if he thinks fit, make an interim award, and any reference in this Part of this Act to an award includes a reference to an interim award.

Specific performance.
15. Unless a contrary intention is expressed therein, every arbitration agreement shall, where such a provision is applicable to the reference, be deemed to contain a provision that the arbitrator or umpire shall have the same power as the High Court to order specific performance of any contract other than a contract relating to land or any interest in land.

16. Unless a contrary intention is expressed therein, every arbitration agreement shall, where such a provision is applicable to the reference, be deemed to contain a provision that the award to be made by the arbitrator or umpire shall be final and binding on the parties and the persons claiming under them respectively.

<small>PART I
—cont.
Awards to be final.</small>

17. Unless a contrary intention is expressed in the arbitration agreement, the arbitrator or umpire shall have power to correct in an award any clerical mistake or error arising from any accidental slip or omission.

<small>Power to correct slips.</small>

Costs, Fees and Interest

18.—(1) Unless a contrary intention is expressed therein, every arbitration agreement shall be deemed to include a provision that the costs of the reference and award shall be in the discretion of the arbitrator or umpire, who may direct to and by whom and in what manner those costs or any part thereof shall be paid, and may tax or settle the amount of costs to be so paid or any part thereof, and may award costs to be paid as between solicitor and client.

<small>Costs.</small>

(2) Any costs directed by an award to be paid shall, unless the award otherwise directs, be taxable in the High Court.

(3) Any provision in an arbitration agreement to the effect that the parties or any party thereto shall in any event pay their or his own costs of the reference or award or any part thereof shall be void, and this Part of this Act shall, in the case of an arbitration agreement containing any such provision, have effect as if that provision were not contained therein:

Provided that nothing in this subsection shall invalidate such a provision when it is a part of an agreement to submit to arbitration a dispute which has arisen before the making of that agreement.

(4) If no provision is made by an award with respect to the costs of the reference, any party to the reference may, within fourteen days of the publication of the award or such further time as the High Court or a judge thereof may direct, apply to the arbitrator for an order directing by and to whom those costs shall be paid, and thereupon the arbitrator shall, after hearing any party who may desire to be heard, amend his award by adding thereto such directions as he may think proper with respect to the payment of the costs of the reference.

(5) Section sixty-nine of the Solicitors Act, 1932 (which empowers a court before which any proceeding is being heard or is pending to charge property recovered or preserved in the

Part I
—cont.

proceeding with the payment of solicitors' costs) shall apply as if an arbitration were a proceeding in the High Court, and the High Court may make declarations and orders accordingly.

Taxation of arbitrator's or umpire's fees.

19.—(1) If in any case an arbitrator or umpire refuses to deliver his award except on payment of the fees demanded by him, the High Court may, on an application for the purpose, order that the arbitrator or umpire shall deliver the award to the applicant on payment into court by the applicant of the fees demanded, and further that the fees demanded shall be taxed by the taxing officer and that out of the money paid into court there shall be paid out to the arbitrator or umpire by way of fees such sum as may be found reasonable on taxation and that the balance of the money, if any, shall be paid out to the applicant.

(2) An application for the purposes of this section may be made by any party to the reference unless the fees demanded have been fixed by a written agreement between him and the arbitrator or umpire.

(3) A taxation of fees under this section may be reviewed in the same manner as a taxation of costs.

(4) The arbitrator or umpire shall be entitled to appear and be heard on any taxation or review of taxation under this section.

Interest on awards.

20. A sum directed to be paid by an award shall, unless the award otherwise directs, carry interest as from the date of the award and at the same rate as a judgment debt.

Special Cases, Remission and Setting aside of Awards, &c.

Statement of case.
REPEALED

21.—(1) An arbitrator or umpire may, and shall if so directed by the High Court, state—

(a) any question of law arising in the course of the reference; or

(b) an award or any part of an award,

in the form of a special case for the decision of the High Court.

(2) A special case with respect to an interim award or with respect to a question of law arising in the course of a reference may be stated, or may be directed by the High Court to be stated, notwithstanding that proceedings under the reference are still pending.

(3) A decision of the High Court under this section shall be deemed to be a judgment of the Court within the meaning of section twenty-seven of the Supreme Court of Judicature (Consolidation) Act, 1925 (which relates to the jurisdiction of the Court of Appeal to hear and determine appeals from any judgment of the High Court), but no appeal shall lie from the

~~decision of the High Court on any case stated under paragraph~~
(*a*) of subsection (1) ~~of this section~~ without the leave of the
~~High Court or of the Court of Appeal~~.

PART I
—*cont*.

22.—(1) In all cases of reference to arbitration the High Court or a judge thereof may from time to time remit the matters referred, or any of them, to the reconsideration of the arbitrator or umpire.

Power to remit award.

(2) Where an award is remitted, the arbitrator or umpire shall, unless the order otherwise directs, make his award within three months after the date of the order.

23.—(1) Where an arbitrator or umpire has misconducted himself or the proceedings, the High Court may remove him.

Removal of arbitrator and setting aside of award.

(2) Where an arbitrator or umpire has misconducted himself or the proceedings, or an arbitration or award has been improperly procured, the High Court may set the award aside.

(3) Where an application is made to set aside an award, the High Court may order that any money made payable by the award shall be brought into court or otherwise secured pending the determination of the application.

24.—(1) Where an agreement between any parties provides that disputes which may arise in the future between them shall be referred to an arbitrator named or designated in the agreement, and after a dispute has arisen any party applies, on the ground that the arbitrator so named or designated is not or may not be impartial, for leave to revoke the authority of the arbitrator or for an injunction to restrain any other party or the arbitrator from proceeding with the arbitration, it shall not be a ground for refusing the application that the said party at the time when he made the agreement knew, or ought to have known, that the arbitrator, by reason of his relation towards any other party to the agreement or of his connection with the subject referred, might not be capable of impartiality.

Power of court to give relief where arbitrator is not impartial or the dispute involves question of fraud.

(2) Where an agreement between any parties provides that disputes which may arise in the future between them shall be referred to arbitration, and a dispute which so arises involves the question whether any such party has been guilty of fraud, the High Court shall, so far as may be necessary to enable that question to be determined by the High Court, have power to order that the agreement shall cease to have effect and power to give leave to revoke the authority of any arbitrator or umpire appointed by or by virtue of the agreement.

(3) In any case where by virtue of this section the High Court has power to order that an arbitration agreement shall cease to have effect or to give leave to revoke the authority of an arbitrator or umpire, the High Court may refuse to stay any action brought in breach of the agreement.

PART I
—*cont.*

Power of court where arbitrator is removed or authority of arbitrator is revoked.

25.—(1) Where an arbitrator (not being a sole arbitrator), or two or more arbitrators (not being all the arbitrators) or an umpire who has not entered on the reference is or are removed by the High Court, the High Court may, on the application of any party to the arbitration agreement, appoint a person or persons to act as arbitrator or arbitrators or umpire in place of the person or persons so removed.

(2) Where the authority of an arbitrator or arbitrators or umpire is revoked by leave of the High Court, or a sole arbitrator or all the arbitrators or an umpire who has entered on the reference is or are removed by the High Court, the High Court may, on the application of any party to the arbitration agreement, either—

> (*a*) appoint a person to act as sole arbitrator in place of the person or persons removed ; or
>
> (*b*) order that the arbitration agreement shall cease to have effect with respect to the dispute referred.

(3) A person appointed under this section by the High Court as an arbitrator or umpire shall have the like power to act in the reference and to make an award as if he had been appointed in accordance with the terms of the arbitration agreement.

(4) Where it is provided (whether by means of a provision in the arbitration agreement or otherwise) that an award under an arbitration agreement shall be a condition precedent to the bringing of an action with respect to any matter to which the agreement applies, the High Court, if it orders (whether under this section or under any other enactment) that the agreement shall cease to have effect as regards any particular dispute, may further order that the provision making an award a condition precedent to the bringing of an action shall also cease to have effect as regards that dispute.

Enforcement of Award

Enforcement of award.

26. An award on an arbitration agreement may, by leave of the High Court or a judge thereof, be enforced in the same manner as a judgment or order to the same effect, and where leave is so given, judgment may be entered in terms of the award.

Miscellaneous

Power of court to extend time for commencing arbitration proceedings.

27. Where the terms of an agreement to refer future disputes to arbitration provide that any claims to which the agreement applies shall be barred unless notice to appoint an arbitrator is given or an arbitrator is appointed or some other step to commence arbitration proceedings is taken within a time fixed by the agreement, and a dispute arises to which the agreement applies, the High Court, if it is of opinion that in the circumstances of the case undue hardship would otherwise be caused,

and notwithstanding that the time so fixed has expired, may, on such terms, if any, as the justice of the case may require, but without prejudice to the provisions of any enactment limiting the time for the commencement of arbitration proceedings, extend the time for such period as it thinks proper.

28. Any order made under this Part of this Act may be made on such terms as to costs or otherwise as the authority making the order thinks just:

~~Provided that this section shall not apply to any order made under subsection (2) of section four of this Act.~~

Terms as to costs, &c.

29.—(1) In subsection (3) of section four hundred and ninety-six of the Merchant Shipping Act, 1894 (which requires a sum deposited with a wharfinger by an owner of goods to be repaid unless legal proceedings are instituted by the shipowner), the expression "legal proceedings" shall be deemed to include arbitration.

Extension of s. 496 of the Merchant Shipping Act, 1894.

(2) For the purposes of the said section four hundred and ninety-six, as amended by this section, an arbitration shall be deemed to be commenced when one party to the arbitration agreement serves on the other party or parties a notice requiring him or them to appoint or concur in appointing an arbitrator, or, where the arbitration agreement provides that the reference shall be to a person named or designated in the agreement, requiring him or them to submit the dispute to the person so named or designated.

(3) Any such notice as is mentioned in subsection (2) of this section may be served either—
  (a) by delivering it to the person on whom it is to be served ; or
  (b) by leaving it at the usual or last known place of abode in England of that person ; or
  (c) by sending it by post in a registered letter addressed to that person at his usual or last known place of abode in England ;

as well as in any other manner provided in the arbitration agreement ; and where a notice is sent by post in manner prescribed by paragraph (c) of this subsection, service thereof shall, unless the contrary is proved, be deemed to have been effected at the time at which the letter would have been delivered in the ordinary course of post.

30. This Part of this Act (~~except the provisions of subsection (2) of section four thereof~~) shall apply to any arbitration to which His Majesty, either in right of the Crown or of the Duchy of Lancaster or otherwise, or the Duke of Cornwall, is a party.

Crown to be bound.

PART I
—cont.

Application of Part I to statutory arbitrations.

31.—(1) Subject to the provisions of section thirty-three of this Act, this Part of this Act, except the provisions thereof specified in subsection (2) of this section, shall apply to every arbitration under any other Act (whether passed before or after the commencement of this Act) as if the arbitration were pursuant to an arbitration agreement and as if that other Act were an arbitration agreement, except in so far as this Act is inconsistent with that other Act or with any rules or procedure authorised or recognised thereby.

(2) The provisions referred to in subsection (1) of this section are subsection (1) of section two, section three, ~~subsection (2) of section four~~, section five, subsection (3) of section eighteen and sections twenty-four, twenty-five, twenty-seven and twenty-nine.

Meaning of "arbitration agreement"

32. In this Part of this Act, unless the context otherwise requires, the expression "arbitration agreement" means a written agreement to submit present or future differences to arbitration, whether an arbitrator is named therein or not.

Operation of Part I.

33. This Part of this Act shall not affect any arbitration commenced (within the meaning of subsection (2) of section twenty-nine of this Act) before the commencement of this Act, but shall apply to an arbitration so commenced after the commencement of this Act under an agreement made before the commencement of this Act.

Extent of Part I.

34. ~~Subsection (2) of section four of this Act shall—~~

(a) extend to Scotland, with the omission of the words "Notwithstanding anything in this Part of this Act" and with the substitution, for references to staying proceedings, of references to sisting proceedings; and

(b) extend to Northern Ireland, with the omission of the words "Notwithstanding anything in this Part of this Act";

~~but, save as aforesaid,~~ None of the provisions of this Part of this Act shall extend to Scotland or Northern Ireland.

PART II

ENFORCEMENT OF CERTAIN FOREIGN AWARDS

Awards to which Part II applies.

35.—(1) This Part of this Act applies to any award made after the twenty-eighth day of July, nineteen hundred and twenty-four—

(a) in pursuance of an agreement for arbitration to which the protocol set out in the First Schedule to this Act applies; and

(b) between persons of whom one is subject to the jurisdiction of some one of such Powers as His Majesty, being satisfied that reciprocal provisions have been made, may by Order in Council declare to be parties to the convention set out in the Second Schedule to this Act, and of whom the other is subject to the jurisdiction of some other of the Powers aforesaid ; and

(c) in one of such territories as His Majesty, being satisfied that reciprocal provisions have been made, may by Order in Council declare to be territories to which the the said convention applies ;

and an award to which this Part of this Act applies is in this Part of this Act referred to as " a foreign award ".

(2) His Majesty may by a subsequent Order in Council vary or revoke any Order previously made under this section.

(3) Any Order in Council under section one of the Arbitration (Foreign Awards) Act, 1930, which is in force at the commencement of this Act shall have effect as if it had been made under this section.

36.—(1) A foreign award shall, subject to the provisions of this Part of this Act, be enforceable in England either by action or in the same manner as the award of an arbitrator is enforceable by virtue of section twenty-six of this Act.

Effect of foreign awards.

(2) Any foreign award which would be enforceable under this Part of this Act shall be treated as binding for all purposes on the persons as between whom it was made, and may accordingly be relied on by any of those persons by way of defence, set off or otherwise in any legal proceedings in England, and any references in this Part of this Act to enforcing a foreign award shall be construed as including references to relying on an award.

37.—(1) In order that a foreign award may be enforceable under this Part of this Act it must have—

Conditions for enforcement of foreign awards.

(a) been made in pursuance of an agreement for arbitration which was valid under the law by which it was governed ;

(b) been made by the tribunal provided for in the agreement or constituted in manner agreed upon by the parties ;

(c) been made in conformity with the law governing the arbitration procedure ;

(d) become final in the country in which it was made ;

(e) been in respect of a matter which may lawfully be referred to arbitration under the law of England ;

and the enforcement thereof must not be contrary to the public policy or the law of England.

(2) Subject to the provisions of this subsection, a foreign award shall not be enforceable under this Part of this Act if the court dealing with the case is satisfied that—

(a) the award has been annulled in the country in which it was made ; or

PART II
—cont.

 (b) the party against whom it is sought to enforce the award was not given notice of the arbitration proceedings in sufficient time to enable him to present his case, or was under some legal incapacity and was not properly represented ; or

 (c) the award does not deal with all the questions referred or contains decisions on matters beyond the scope of the agreement for arbitration :

Provided that, if the award does not deal with all the questions referred, the court may, if it thinks fit, either postpone the enforcement of the award or order its enforcement subject to the giving of such security by the person seeking to enforce it as the court may think fit.

(3) If a party seeking to resist the enforcement of a foreign award proves that there is any ground other than the non-existence of the conditions specified in paragraphs (a), (b) and (c) of subsection (1) of this section, or the existence of the conditions specified in paragraphs (b) and (c) of subsection (2) of this section, entitling him to contest the validity of the award, the court may, if it thinks fit, either refuse to enforce the award or adjourn the hearing until after the expiration of such period as appears to the court to be reasonably sufficient to enable that party to take the necessary steps to have the award annulled by the competent tribunal.

Evidence.

38.—(1) The party seeking to enforce a foreign award must produce—

 (a) the original award or a copy thereof duly authenticated in manner required by the law of the country in which it was made ; and

 (b) evidence proving that the award has become final ; and

 (c) such evidence as may be necessary to prove that the award is a foreign award and that the conditions mentioned in paragraphs (a), (b) and (c) of subsection (1) of the last foregoing section are satisfied.

(2) In any case where any document required to be produced under subsection (1) of this section is in a foreign language, it shall be the duty of the party seeking to enforce the award to produce a translation certified as correct by a diplomatic or consular agent of the country to which that party belongs, or certified as correct in such other manner as may be sufficient according to the law of England.

(3) Subject to the provisions of this section, rules of court may be made under section ninety-nine of the Supreme Court of Judicature (Consolidation) Act, 1925, with respect to the evidence which must be furnished by a party seeking to enforce an award under this Part of this Act.

39. For the purposes of this Part of this Act, an award shall not be deemed final if any proceedings for the purpose of contesting the validity of the award are pending in the country in which it was made.

PART II
—*cont.*

Meaning of "final award".

40. Nothing in this Part of this Act shall—
  (*a*) prejudice any rights which any person would have had of enforcing in England any award or of availing himself in England of any award if neither this Part of this Act nor Part I of the Arbitration (Foreign Awards) Act. 1930, had been enacted; or
  (*b*) apply to any award made on an arbitration agreement governed by the law of England.

Saving for other rights, &c.

41.—(1) The following provisions of this section shall have effect for the purpose of the application of this Part of this Act to Scotland.

Application of Part II to Scotland.

(2) For the references to England there shall be substituted references to Scotland.

(3) For subsection (1) of section thirty-six there shall be substituted the following subsection:—

  "(1) A foreign award shall, subject to the provisions of this Part of this Act, be enforceable by action, or, if the agreement for arbitration contains consent to the registration of the award in the Books of Council and Session for execution and the award is so registered, it shall, subject as aforesaid, be enforceable by summary diligence".

(4) For subsection (3) of section thirty-eight there shall be substituted the following subsection:—

  "(3) The Court of Session shall, subject to the provisions of this section, have power, exercisable by statutory instrument, to make provision by Act of Sederunt with respect to the evidence which must be furnished by a party seeking to enforce in Scotland an award under this Part of this Act, and the Statutory Instruments Act, 1946, shall apply to a statutory instrument containing an Act of Sederunt made under this subsection as if the Act of Sederunt had been made by a Minister of the Crown".

42.—(1) The following provisions of this section shall have effect for the purpose of the application of this Part of this Act to Northern Ireland.

Application of Part II to Northern Ireland.

(2) For the references to England there shall be substituted references to Northern Ireland.

PART II
—*cont.*

(3) For subsection (1) of section thirty-six there shall be substituted the following subsection:—

"(1) A foreign award shall, subject to the provisions of this Part of this Act, be enforceable either by action or in the same manner as the award of an arbitrator under the provisions of the Common Law Procedure Amendment Act (Ireland), 1856, was enforceable at the date of the passing of the Arbitration (Foreign Awards) Act, 1930".

(4) For the reference, in subsection (3) of section thirty-eight, to section ninety-nine of the Supreme Court of Judicature (Consolidation) Act, 1925, there shall be substituted a reference to section sixty-one of the Supreme Court of Judicature (Ireland) Act, 1877, as amended by any subsequent enactment.

Saving for pending proceedings.

43. Any proceedings instituted under Part I of the Arbitration (Foreign Awards) Act, 1930, which are uncompleted at the commencement of this Act may be carried on and completed under this Part of this Act as if they had been instituted thereunder.

PART III

GENERAL

Short title, commencement and repeal.

44.—(1) This Act may be cited as the Arbitration Act, 1950.

(2) This Act shall come into operation on the first day of September, nineteen hundred and fifty.

(3) The Arbitration Act, 1889, the Arbitration Clauses (Protocol) Act, 1924, and the Arbitration Act, 1934, are hereby repealed except in relation to arbitrations commenced (within the meaning of subsection (2) of section twenty-nine of this Act) before the commencement of this Act, and the Arbitration (Foreign Awards) Act, 1930, is hereby repealed; and any reference in any Act or other document to any enactment hereby repealed shall be construed as including a reference to the corresponding provision of this Act.

SCHEDULES

FIRST SCHEDULE

Sections 4, 35.

PROTOCOL ON ARBITRATION CLAUSES SIGNED ON BEHALF OF HIS MAJESTY AT A MEETING OF THE ASSEMBLY OF THE LEAGUE OF NATIONS HELD ON THE TWENTY-FOURTH DAY OF SEPTEMBER, NINETEEN HUNDRED AND TWENTY-THREE

The undersigned, being duly authorised, declare that they accept, on behalf of the countries which they represent, the following provisions:—

1. Each of the Contracting States recognises the validity of an agreement whether relating to existing or future differences between parties, subject respectively to the jurisdiction of different Contracting States by which the parties to a contract agree to submit to arbitration all or any differences that may arise in connection with such contract relating to commercial matters or to any other matter capable of settlement by arbitration, whether or not the arbitration is to take place in a country to whose jurisdiction none of the parties is subject.

Each Contracting State reserves the right to limit the obligation mentioned above to contracts which are considered as commercial under its national law. Any Contracting State which avails itself of this right will notify the Secretary-General of the League of Nations, in order that the other Contracting States may be so informed.

2. The arbitral procedure, including the constitution of the arbitral tribunal, shall be governed by the will of the parties and by the law of the country in whose territory the arbitration takes place.

The Contracting States agree to facilitate all steps in the procedure which require to be taken in their own territories, in accordance with the provisions of their law governing arbitral procedure applicable to existing differences.

3. Each Contracting State undertakes to ensure the execution by its authorities and in accordance with the provisions of its national laws of arbitral awards made in its own territory under the preceding articles.

4. The tribunals of the Contracting Parties, on being seized of a dispute regarding a contract made between persons to whom Article 1 applies and including an arbitration agreement whether referring to present or future differences which is valid in virtue of the said article and capable of being carried into effect, shall refer the parties on the application of either of them to the decision of the arbitrators.

Such reference shall not prejudice the competence of the judicial tribunals in case the agreement or the arbitration cannot proceed or become inoperative.

5. The present Protocol, which shall remain open for signature by all States, shall be ratified. The ratifications shall be deposited as soon as possible with the Secretary-General of the League of Nations, who shall notify such deposit to all the signatory States.

1ST SCH.
—cont.

6. The present Protocol shall come into force as soon as two ratifications have been deposited. Thereafter it will take effect, in the case of each Contracting State, one month after the notification by the Secretary-General of the deposit of its ratification.

7. The present Protocol may be denounced by any Contracting State on giving one year's notice. Denunciation shall be effected by a notification addressed to the Secretary-General of the League, who will immediately transmit copies of such notification to all the other signatory States and inform them of the date of which it was received. The denunciation shall take effect one year after the date on which it was notified to the Secretary-General, and shall operate only in respect of the notifying State.

8. The Contracting States may declare that their acceptance of the present Protocol does not include any or all of the under-mentioned territories: that is to say, their colonies, overseas possessions or territories, protectorates or the territories over which they exercise a mandate.

The said States may subsequently adhere separately on behalf of any territory thus excluded. The Secretary-General of the League of Nations shall be informed as soon as possible of such adhesions. He shall notify such adhesions to all signatory States. They will take effect one month after the notification by the Secretary-General to all signatory States.

The Contracting States may also denounce the Protocol separately on behalf of any of the territories referred to above. Article 7 applies to such denunciation.

Section 35.

SECOND SCHEDULE

CONVENTION ON THE EXECUTION OF FOREIGN ARBITRAL AWARDS SIGNED AT GENEVA ON BEHALF OF HIS MAJESTY ON THE TWENTY-SIXTH DAY OF SEPTEMBER, NINETEEN HUNDRED AND TWENTY-SEVEN

ARTICLE I

In the territories of any High Contracting Party to which the present Convention applies, an arbitral award made in pursuance of an agreement, whether relating to existing or future differences (hereinafter called "a submission to arbitration") covered by the Protocol on Arbitration Clauses, opened at Geneva on September 24, 1923, shall be recognised as binding and shall be enforced in accordance with the rules of the procedure of the territory where the award is relied upon, provided that the said award has been made in a territory of one of the High Contracting Parties to which the present Convention applies and between persons who are subject to the jurisdiction of one of the High Contracting Parties.

To obtain such recognition or enforcement, it shall, further, be necessary:—

    (a) That the award has been made in pursuance of a submission to arbitration which is valid under the law applicable thereto;

(b) That the subject-matter of the award is capable of settlement by arbitration under the law of the country in which the award is sought to be relied upon ;
(c) That the award has been made by the Arbitral Tribunal provided for in the submission to arbitration or constituted in the manner agreed upon by the parties and in conformity with the law governing the arbitration procedure ;
(d) That the award has become final in the country in which it has been made, in the sense that it will not be considered as such if it is open to *opposition, appel* or *pourvoi en cassation* (in the countries where such forms of procedure exist) or if it is proved that any proceedings for the purpose of contesting the validity of the award are pending ;
(e) That the recognition or enforcement of the award is not contrary to the public policy or to the principles of the law of the country in which it is sought to be relied upon.

Article 2

Even if the conditions laid down in Article 1 hereof are fulfilled, recognition and enforcement of the award shall be refused if the Court is satisfied : —
(a) That the award has been annulled in the country in which it was made ;
(b) That the party against whom it is sought to use the award was not given notice of the arbitration proceedings in sufficient time to enable him to present his case ; or that, being under a legal incapacity, he was not properly represented ;
(c) That the award does not deal with the differences contemplated by or falling within the terms of the submission to arbitration or that it contains decisions on matters beyond the scope of the submission to arbitration.

If the award has not covered all the questions submitted to the arbitral tribunal, the competent authority of the country where recognition or enforcement of the award is sought can, if it think fit, postpone such recognition or enforcement or grant it subject to such guarantee as that authority may decide.

Article 3

If the party against whom the award has been made proves that, under the law governing the arbitration procedure, there is a ground, other than the grounds referred to in Article 1 (a) and (c), and Article 2 (b) and (c), entitling him to contest the validity of the award in a Court of Law, the Court may, if it thinks fit, either refuse recognition or enforcement of the award or adjourn the consideration thereof, giving such party a reasonable time within which to have the award annulled by the competent tribunal.

Article 4

The party relying upon an award or claiming its enforcement must supply, in particular: —
  (1) The original award or a copy thereof duly authenticated, according to the requirements of the law of the country in which it was made;
  (2) Documentary or other evidence to prove that the award has become final, in the sense defined in Article 1 (*d*), in the country in which it was made;
  (3) When necessary, documentary or other evidence to prove that the conditions laid down in Article 1, paragraph 1 and paragraph 2 (*a*) and (*c*), have been fulfilled.

A translation of the award and of the other documents mentioned in this Article into the official language of the country where the award is sought to be relied upon may be demanded. Such translation must be certified correct by a diplomatic or consular agent of the country to which the party who seeks to rely upon the award belongs or by a sworn translator of the country where the award is sought to be relied upon.

Article 5

The provisions of the above Articles shall not deprive any interested party of the right of availing himself of an arbitral award in the manner and to the extent allowed by the law or the treaties of the country where such award is sought to be relied upon.

Article 6

The present Convention applies only to arbitral awards made after the coming into force of the Protocol on Arbitration Clauses, opened at Geneva on September 24th, 1923.

Article 7

The present Convention, which will remain open to the signature of all the signatories of the Protocol of 1923 on Arbitration Clauses, shall be ratified.

It may be ratified only on behalf of those Members of the League of Nations and non-Member States on whose behalf the Protocol of 1923 shall have been ratified.

Ratifications shall be deposited as soon as possible with the Secretary-General of the League of Nations, who will notify such deposit to all the signatories.

Article 8

The present Convention shall come into force three months after it shall have been ratified on behalf of two High Contracting Parties. Thereafter, it shall take effect, in the case of each High Contracting Party, three months after the deposit of the ratification on its behalf with the Secretary-General of the League of Nations.

Article 9

The present Convention may be denounced on behalf of any Member of the League or non-Member State. Denunciation shall be notified in writing to the Secretary-General of the League of Nations, who will immediately send a copy thereof, certified to be in conformity with the notification, to all the other Contracting Parties, at the same time informing them of the date on which he received it.

The denunciation shall come into force only in respect of the High Contracting Party which shall have notified it and one year after such notification shall have reached the Secretary-General of the League of Nations.

The denunciation of the Protocol on Arbitration Clauses shall entail, ipso facto, the denunciation of the present Convention.

Article 10

The present Convention does not apply to the Colonies, Protectorates or territories under suzerainty or mandate of any High Contracting Party unless they are specially mentioned.

The application of this Convention to one or more of such Colonies, Protectorates or territories to which the Protocol on Arbitration Clauses, opened at Geneva on September 24th, 1923, applies, can be effected at any time by means of a declaration addressed to the Secretary-General of the League of Nations by one of the High Contracting Parties.

Such declaration shall take effect three months after the deposit thereof.

The High Contracting Parties can at any time denounce the Convention for all or any of the Colonies, Protectorates or territories referred to above. Article 9 hereof applies to such denunciation.

Article 11

A certified copy of the present Convention shall be transmitted by the Secretary-General of the League of Nations to every Member of the League of Nations and to every non-Member State which signs the same.

2ND SCH.
—cont.

Table of Statutes referred to in this Act

Short Title	Session and Chapter
Common Law Procedure Amendment Act (Ireland), 1856	19 & 20 Vict. c. 102.
Supreme Court of Judicature (Ireland) Act, 1877	40 & 41 Vict. c. 57.
Arbitration Act, 1889	52 & 53 Vict. c. 49.
Merchant Shipping Act, 1894	57 & 58 Vict. c. 60.
Arbitration Clauses (Protocol) Act, 1924	14 & 15 Geo. 5. c. 39.
Supreme Court of Judicature (Consolidation) Act, 1925	15 & 16 Geo. 5. c. 49.
Arbitration (Foreign Awards) Act, 1930	20 Geo. 5. c. 15.
Arbitration Act, 1934	24 & 25 Geo. 5. c. 14.
Statutory Instruments Act, 1946	9 & 10 Geo. 6. c. 36.

Arbitration Act 1975

1975 CHAPTER 3

An Act to give effect to the New York Convention on the Recognition and Enforcement of Foreign Arbitral Awards. [25th February 1975]

BE IT ENACTED by the Queen's most Excellent Majesty, by and with the advice and consent of the Lords Spiritual and Temporal, and Commons, in this present Parliament assembled, and by the authority of the same, as follows:—

Effect of arbitration agreement on court proceedings

1.—(1) If any party to an arbitration agreement to which this section applies, or any person claiming through or under him, commences any legal proceedings in any court against any other party to the agreement, or any person claiming through or under him, in respect of any matter agreed to be referred, any party to the proceedings may at any time after appearance, and before delivering any pleadings or taking any other steps in the proceedings, apply to the court to stay the proceedings; and the court, unless satisfied that the arbitration agreement is null and void, inoperative or incapable of being performed or that there is not in fact any dispute between the parties with regard to the matter agreed to be referred, shall make an order staying the proceedings. *[Staying court proceedings where party proves arbitration agreement.]*

(2) This section applies to any arbitration agreement which is not a domestic arbitration agreement; and neither section 4(1) of the Arbitration Act 1950 nor section 4 of the Arbitration Act (Northern Ireland) 1937 shall apply to an arbitration agreement to which this section applies. *[1950 c. 27. 1937 c. 8 (N.I.).]*

(3) In the application of this section to Scotland, for the references to staying proceedings there shall be substituted references to sisting proceedings.

(4) In this section "domestic arbitration agreement" means an arbitration agreement which does not provide, expressly or by implication, for arbitration in a State other than the United Kingdom and to which neither—

    (a) an individual who is a national of, or habitually resident in, any State other than the United Kingdom; nor

    (b) a body corporate which is incorporated in, or whose central management and control is exercised in, any State other than the United Kingdom;

is a party at the time the proceedings are commenced.

Enforcement of Convention awards

Replacement of former provisions.
1950 c. 27.

2. Sections 3 to 6 of this Act shall have effect with respect to the enforcement of Convention awards; and where a Convention award would, but for this section, be also a foreign award within the meaning of Part II of the Arbitration Act 1950, that Part shall not apply to it.

Effect of Convention awards.

3.—(1) A Convention award shall, subject to the following provisions of this Act, be enforceable—

    (a) in England and Wales, either by action or in the same manner as the award of an arbitrator is enforceable by virtue of section 26 of the Arbitration Act 1950;

    (b) in Scotland, either by action or, in a case where the arbitration agreement contains consent to the registration of the award in the Books of Council and Session for execution and the award is so registered, by summary diligence;

1937 c. 8 (N.I.).

    (c) in Northern Ireland, either by action or in the same manner as the award of an arbitrator is enforceable by virtue of section 16 of the Arbitration Act (Northern Ireland) 1937.

(2) Any Convention award which would be enforceable under this Act shall be treated as binding for all purposes on the persons as between whom it was made, and may accordingly be relied on by any of those persons by way of defence, set off or otherwise in any legal proceedings in the United Kingdom; and any reference in this Act to enforcing a Convention award shall be construed as including references to relying on such an award.

Evidence.

4. The party seeking to enforce a Convention award must produce—

    (a) the duly authenticated original award or a duly certified copy of it; and

(b) the original arbitration agreement or a duly certified copy of it ; and

(c) where the award or agreement is in a foreign language, a translation of it certified by an official or sworn translator or by a diplomatic or consular agent.

5.—(1) Enforcement of a Convention award shall not be refused except in the cases mentioned in this section. <small>Refusal of enforcement.</small>

(2) Enforcement of a Convention award may be refused if the person against whom it is invoked proves—

(a) that a party to the arbitration agreement was (under the law applicable to him) under some incapacity ; or

(b) that the arbitration agreement was not valid under the law to which the parties subjected it or, failing any indication thereon, under the law of the country where the award was made ; or

(c) that he was not given proper notice of the appointment of the arbitrator or of the arbitration proceedings or was otherwise unable to present his case ; or

(d) (subject to subsection (4) of this section) that the award deals with a difference not contemplated by or not falling within the terms of the submission to arbitration or contains decisions on matters beyond the scope of the submission to arbitration ; or

(e) that the composition of the arbitral authority or the arbitral procedure was not in accordance with the agreement of the parties or, failing such agreement, with the law of the country where the arbitration took place ; or

(f) that the award has not yet become binding on the parties, or has been set aside or suspended by a competent authority of the country in which, or under the law of which, it was made.

(3) Enforcement of a Convention award may also be refused if the award is in respect of a matter which is not capable of settlement by arbitration, or if it would be contrary to public policy to enforce the award.

(4) A Convention award which contains decisions on matters not submitted to arbitration may be enforced to the extent that it contains decisions on matters submitted to arbitration which can be separated from those on matters not so submitted.

(5) Where an application for the setting aside or suspension of a Convention award has been made to such a competent authority as is mentioned in subsection (2)(f) of this section, the

court before which enforcement of the award is sought may, if it thinks fit, adjourn the proceedings and may, on the application of the party seeking to enforce the award, order the other party to give security.

Saving

1950 c. 27.

6. Nothing in this Act shall prejudice any right to enforce or rely on an award otherwise than under this Act or Part II of the Arbitration Act 1950.

General

Interpretation.

7.—(1) In this Act—

"arbitration agreement" means an agreement in writing (including an agreement contained in an exchange of letters or telegrams) to submit to arbitration present or future differences capable of settlement by arbitration;

"Convention award" means an award made in pursuance of an arbitration agreement in the territory of a State, other than the United Kingdom, which is a party to the New York Convention; and

"the New York Convention" means the Convention on the Recognition and Enforcement of Foreign Arbitral Awards adopted by the United Nations Conference on International Commercial Arbitration on 10th June 1958.

(2) If Her Majesty by Order in Council declares that any State specified in the Order is a party to the New York Convention the Order shall, while in force, be conclusive evidence that that State is a party to that Convention.

(3) An Order in Council under this section may be varied or revoked by a subsequent Order in Council.

Short title, repeals, commencement and extent.

8.—(1) This Act may be cited as the Arbitration Act 1975.

(2) The following provisions of the Arbitration Act 1950 are hereby repealed, that is to say—

(a) section 4(2);

(b) in section 28 the proviso;

(c) in section 30 the words "(except the provisions of sub-section (2) of section 4 thereof)";

(d) in section 31(2) the words "subsection (2) of section 4"; and

(e) in section 34 the words from the beginning to "save as aforesaid".

(3) This Act shall come into operation on such date as the Secretary of State may by order made by statutory instrument appoint.

(4) This Act extends to Northern Ireland.

Arbitration Act 1979

1979 CHAPTER 42

An Act to amend the law relating to arbitrations and for purposes connected therewith. [4th April 1979]

BE IT ENACTED by the Queen's most Excellent Majesty, by and with the advice and consent of the Lords Spiritual and Temporal, and Commons, in this present Parliament assembled, and by the authority of the same, as follows:—

1.—(1) In the Arbitration Act 1950 (in this Act referred to as "the principal Act") section 21 (statement of case for a decision of the High Court) shall cease to have effect and, without prejudice to the right of appeal conferred by subsection (2) below, the High Court shall not have jurisdiction to set aside or remit an award on an arbitration agreement on the ground of errors of fact or law on the face of the award. *Judicial review of arbitration awards. 1950 c. 27.*

(2) Subject to subsection (3) below, an appeal shall lie to the High Court on any question of law arising out of an award made on an arbitration agreement; and on the determination of such an appeal the High Court may by order—

    (*a*) confirm, vary or set aside the award; or

    (*b*) remit the award to the reconsideration of the arbitrator or umpire together with the court's opinion on the question of law which was the subject of the appeal;

and where the award is remitted under paragraph (*b*) above the arbitrator or umpire shall, unless the order otherwise directs, make his award within three months after the date of the order.

(3) An appeal under this section may be brought by any of the parties to the reference—

   (*a*) with the consent of all the other parties to the reference; or

   (*b*) subject to section 3 below, with the leave of the court.

(4) The High Court shall not grant leave under subsection (3)(*b*) above unless it considers that, having regard to all the circumstances, the determination of the question of law concerned could substantially affect the rights of one or more of the parties to the arbitration agreement; and the court may make any leave which it gives conditional upon the applicant complying with such conditions as it considers appropriate.

(5) Subject to subsection (6) below, if an award is made and, on an application made by any of the parties to the reference,—

   (*a*) with the consent of all the other parties to the reference, or

   (*b*) subject to section 3 below, with the leave of the court,

it appears to the High Court that the award does not or does not sufficiently set out the reasons for the award, the court may order the arbitrator or umpire concerned to state the reasons for his award in sufficient detail to enable the court, should an appeal be brought under this section, to consider any question of law arising out of the award.

(6) In any case where an award is made without any reason being given, the High Court shall not make an order under subsection (5) above unless it is satisfied—

   (*a*) that before the award was made one of the parties to the reference gave notice to the arbitrator or umpire concerned that a reasoned award would be required; or

   (*b*) that there is some special reason why such a notice was not given.

(7) No appeal shall lie to the Court of Appeal from a decision of the High Court on an appeal under this section unless—

   (*a*) the High Court or the Court of Appeal gives leave; and

   (*b*) it is certified by the High Court that the question of law to which its decision relates either is one of general public importance or is one which for some other special reason should be considered by the Court of Appeal.

(8) Where the award of an arbitrator or umpire is varied on appeal, the award as varied shall have effect (except for the purposes of this section) as if it were the award of the arbitrator or umpire.

2.—(1) Subject to subsection (2) and section 3 below, on an application to the High Court made by any of the parties to a reference— *(Determination of preliminary point of law by court.)*
    (a) with the consent of an arbitrator who has entered on the reference or, if an umpire has entered on the reference, with his consent, or
    (b) with the consent of all the other parties,

the High Court shall have jurisdiction to determine any question of law arising in the course of the reference.

(2) The High Court shall not entertain an application under subsection (1)(a) above with respect to any question of law unless it is satisfied that—
    (a) the determination of the application might produce substantial savings in costs to the parties; and
    (b) the question of law is one in respect of which leave to appeal would be likely to be given under section 1(3)(b) above.

(3) A decision of the High Court under this section shall be deemed to be a judgment of the court within the meaning of section 27 of the Supreme Court of Judicature (Consolidation) Act 1925 (appeals to the Court of Appeal), but no appeal shall lie from such a decision unless— *(1925 c. 49.)*
    (a) the High Court or the Court of Appeal gives leave; and
    (b) it is certified by the High Court that the question of law to which its decision relates either is one of general public importance or is one which for some other special reason should be considered by the Court of Appeal.

3.—(1) Subject to the following provisions of this section and section 4 below— *(Exclusion agreements affecting rights under sections 1 and 2.)*
    (a) the High Court shall not, under section 1(3)(b) above, grant leave to appeal with respect to a question of law arising out of an award, and
    (b) the High Court shall not, under section 1(5)(b) above, grant leave to make an application with respect to an award, and
    (c) no application may be made under section 2(1)(a) above with respect to a question of law,

if the parties to the reference in question have entered into an agreement in writing (in this section referred to as an "exclusion agreement") which excludes the right of appeal under section 1 above in relation to that award or, in a case falling within paragraph (c) above, in relation to an award to which the determination of the question of law is material.

(2) An exclusion agreement may be expressed so as to relate to a particular award, to awards under a particular reference or to any other description of awards, whether arising out of the same reference or not; and an agreement may be an exclusion agreement for the purposes of this section whether it is entered into before or after the passing of this Act and whether or not it forms part of an arbitration agreement.

(3) In any case where—
 (a) an arbitration agreement, other than a domestic arbitration agreement, provides for disputes between the parties to be referred to arbitration, and
 (b) a dispute to which the agreement relates involves the question whether a party has been guilty of fraud, and
 (c) the parties have entered into an exclusion agreement which is applicable to any award made on the reference of that dispute,

then, except in so far as the exclusion agreement otherwise provides, the High Court shall not exercise its powers under section 24(2) of the principal Act (to take steps necessary to enable the question to be determined by the High Court) in relation to that dispute.

(4) Except as provided by subsection (1) above, sections 1 and 2 above shall have effect notwithstanding anything in any agreement purporting—
 (a) to prohibit or restrict access to the High Court; or
 (b) to restrict the jurisdiction of that court; or
 (c) to prohibit or restrict the making of a reasoned award.

(5) An exclusion agreement shall be of no effect in relation to an award made on, or a question of law arising in the course of a reference under, a statutory arbitration, that is to say, such an arbitration as is referred to in subsection (1) of section 31 of the principal Act.

(6) An exclusion agreement shall be of no effect in relation to an award made on, or a question of law arising in the course of a reference under, an arbitration agreement which is a domestic arbitration agreement unless the exclusion agreement is entered into after the commencement of the arbitration in which the award is made or, as the case may be, in which the question of law arises.

(7) In this section " domestic arbitration agreement " means an arbitration agreement which does not provide, expressly or by implication, for arbitration in a State other than the United Kingdom and to which neither—
 (a) an individual who is a national of, or habitually resident in, any State other than the United Kingdom, nor

(b) a body corporate which is incorporated in, or whose central management and control is exercised in, any State other than the United Kingdom,

is a party at the time the arbitration agreement is entered into.

4.—(1) Subject to subsection (3) below, if an arbitration award or a question of law arising in the course of a reference relates, in whole or in part, to— *Exclusion agreements not to apply in certain cases.*
 (a) a question or claim falling within the Admiralty jurisdiction of the High Court, or
 (b) a dispute arising out of a contract of insurance, or
 (c) a dispute arising out of a commodity contract,

an exclusion agreement shall have no effect in relation to the award or question unless either—
 (i) the exclusion agreement is entered into after the commencement of the arbitration in which the award is made or, as the case may be, in which the question of law arises, or
 (ii) the award or question relates to a contract which is expressed to be governed by a law other than the law of England and Wales.

(2) In subsection (1)(c) above " commodity contract " means a contract—
 (a) for the sale of goods regularly dealt with on a commodity market or exchange in England or Wales which is specified for the purposes of this section by an order made by the Secretary of State; and
 (b) of a description so specified.

(3) The Secretary of State may by order provide that subsection (1) above—
 (a) shall cease to have effect; or
 (b) subject to such conditions as may be specified in the order, shall not apply to any exclusion agreement made in relation to an arbitration award of a description so specified,

and an order under this subsection may contain such supplementary, incidental and transitional provisions as appear to the Secretary of State to be necessary or expedient.

(4) The power to make an order under subsection (2) or subsection (3) above shall be exercisable by statutory instrument which shall be subject to annulment in pursuance of a resolution of either House of Parliament.

(5) In this section " exclusion agreement " has the same meaning as in section 3 above.

Interlocutory orders.

5.—(1) If any party to a reference under an arbitration agreement fails within the time specified in the order or, if no time is so specified, within a reasonable time to comply with an order made by the arbitrator or umpire in the course of the reference, then, on the application of the arbitrator or umpire or of any party to the reference, the High Court may make an order extending the powers of the arbitrator or umpire as mentioned in subsection (2) below.

(2) If an order is made by the High Court under this section, the arbitrator or umpire shall have power, to the extent and subject to any conditions specified in that order, to continue with the reference in default of appearance or of any other act by one of the parties in like manner as a judge of the High Court might continue with proceedings in that court where a party fails to comply with an order of that court or a requirement of rules of court.

1970 c. 31.

(3) Section 4(5) of the Administration of Justice Act 1970 (jurisdiction of the High Court to be exercisable by the Court of Appeal in relation to judge-arbitrators and judge-umpires) shall not apply in relation to the power of the High Court to make an order under this section, but in the case of a reference to a judge-arbitrator or judge-umpire that power shall be exercisable as in the case of any other reference to arbitration and also by the judge-arbitrator or judge-umpire himself.

(4) Anything done by a judge-arbitrator or judge-umpire in the exercise of the power conferred by subsection (3) above shall be done by him in his capacity as judge of the High Court and have effect as if done by that court.

(5) The preceding provisions of this section have effect notwithstanding anything in any agreement but do not derogate from any powers conferred on an arbitrator or umpire, whether by an arbitration agreement or otherwise.

(6) In this section "judge-arbitrator" and "judge-umpire" have the same meaning as in Schedule 3 to the Administration of Justice Act 1970.

Minor amendments relating to awards and appointment of arbitrators and umpires.

6.—(1) In subsection (1) of section 8 of the principal Act (agreements where reference is to two arbitrators deemed to include provision that the arbitrators shall appoint an umpire immediately after their own appointment)—

    (a) for the words "shall appoint an umpire immediately" there shall be substituted the words "may appoint an umpire at any time"; and

    (b) at the end there shall be added the words "and shall do so forthwith if they cannot agree".

(2) For section 9 of the principal Act (agreements for reference to three arbitrators) there shall be substituted the following section:—

"Majority award of three arbitrators.
9. Unless the contrary intention is expressed in the arbitration agreement, in any case where there is a reference to three arbitrators, the award of any two of the arbitrators shall be binding."

(3) In section 10 of the principal Act (power of court in certain cases to appoint an arbitrator or umpire) in paragraph (c) after the word "are", in the first place where it occurs, there shall be inserted the words "required or are" and the words from "or where" to the end of the paragraph shall be omitted.

(4) At the end of section 10 of the principal Act there shall be added the following subsection:—

" (2) In any case where—

(a) an arbitration agreement provides for the appointment of an arbitrator or umpire by a person who is neither one of the parties nor an existing arbitrator (whether the provision applies directly or in default of agreement by the parties or otherwise), and

(b) that person refuses to make the appointment or does not make it within the time specified in the agreement or, if no time is so specified, within a reasonable time,

any party to the agreement may serve the person in question with a written notice to appoint an arbitrator or umpire and, if the appointment is not made within seven clear days after the service of the notice, the High Court or a judge thereof may, on the application of the party who gave the notice, appoint an arbitrator or umpire who shall have the like powers to act in the reference and make an award as if he had been appointed in accordance with the terms of the agreement."

Application and interpretation of certain provisions of Part I of principal Act.
7.—(1) References in the following provisions of Part I of the principal Act to that Part of that Act shall have effect as if the preceding provisions of this Act were included in that Part, namely,—

(a) section 14 (interim awards);
(b) section 28 (terms as to costs of orders);
(c) section 30 (Crown to be bound);
(d) section 31 (application to statutory arbitrations); and
(e) section 32 (meaning of "arbitration agreement").

(2) Subsections (2) and (3) of section 29 of the principal Act shall apply to determine when an arbitration is deemed to be commenced for the purposes of this Act.

(3) For the avoidance of doubt, it is hereby declared that the reference in subsection (1) of section 31 of the principal Act (statutory arbitrations) to arbitration under any other Act does not extend to arbitration under section 92 of the County Courts Act 1959 (cases in which proceedings are to be or may be referred to arbitration) and accordingly nothing in this Act or in Part I of the principal Act applies to arbitration under the said section 92.

1959 c. 22.

Short title, commencement, repeals and extent.

8.—(1) This Act may be cited as the Arbitration Act 1979.

(2) This Act shall come into operation on such day as the Secretary of State may appoint by order made by statutory instrument; and such an order—

    (a) may appoint different days for different provisions of this Act and for the purposes of the operation of the same provision in relation to different descriptions of arbitration agreement; and

    (b) may contain such supplementary, incidental and transitional provisions as appear to the Secretary of State to be necessary or expedient.

(3) In consequence of the preceding provisions of this Act, the following provisions are hereby repealed, namely—

    (a) in paragraph (c) of section 10 of the principal Act the words from " or where " to the end of the paragraph;

    (b) section 21 of the principal Act;

    (c) in paragraph 9 of Schedule 3 to the Administration of Justice Act 1970, in sub-paragraph (1) the words " 21(1) and (2) " and sub-paragraph (2).

1970 c. 31.

(4) This Act forms part of the law of England and Wales only.

STATUTORY INSTRUMENTS

1979 No. 750 (C.16)

ARBITRATION

The Arbitration Act 1979 (Commencement) Order 1979

Made - - - -   *28th June* 1979

The Secretary of State in exercise of the powers conferred on him by section 8(2) of the Arbitration Act 1979(a) hereby makes the following Order:—

Citation and interpretation

1.—(1) This Order may be cited as the Arbitration Act 1979 (Commencement) Order 1979.

(2) In this Order "the Act" means the Arbitration Act 1979.

Appointed day

2. The Act shall come into operation on 1st August 1979 (hereinafter referred to as "the appointed day"), but, except as provided in Article 3 of this Order, shall not apply to arbitrations commenced before that date.

3. If all the parties to a reference to arbitration commenced before the appointed day have agreed in writing that the Act should apply to that arbitration, the Act shall so apply from the appointed day or the date of the agreement whichever is the later.

Cecil Parkinson,
Minister of State,
28th June 1979.   *Department of Trade.*

EXPLANATORY NOTE

(*This Note is not part of the Order.*)

This Order appoints 1st August 1979 as the day on which the Arbitration Act 1979 ("the Act") comes into operation ("the appointed day").

The Act provides a new system of judicial review of arbitration awards and repeals section 21 of the Arbitration Act 1950 (c. 27) which relates to a statement of a special case for a decision of the High Court, but the Order provides that the Act does not apply to an arbitration commenced before the appointed day, unless the parties agree that it should. Under section 29(2) of the 1950 Act an arbitration is deemed to be commenced when a notice is served by a party to an arbitration agreement requiring the appointment of an arbitrator or requiring the other parties to submit a dispute to an arbitrator designated by the agreement.

Appendix F Flow chart for arbitration

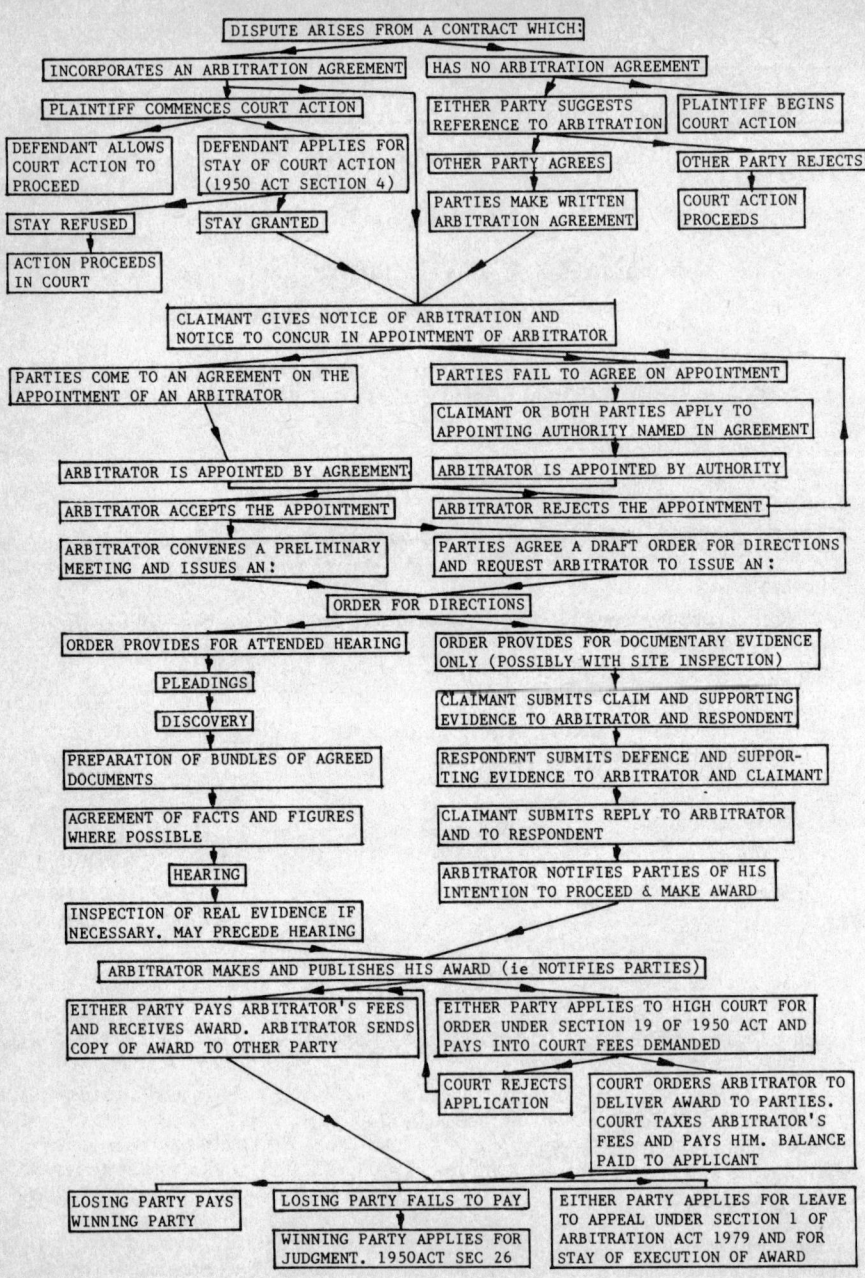

Bibliography

Arbitration
Russell on Arbitration (19th Edn), Anthony Walton, Stevens
Guide to Commercial Arbitration under the 1979 Act, Gibson-Jarvie and Geoffrey Hawker, CIArb
ICE Arbitration Procedure (1973), Institution of Civil Engineers, ICE (under revision)
The Law of Arbitration, W H Gill, Sweet and Maxwell (2nd Edition)
Arbitration Rules (1981 Edn), CIArb
Arbitration for Builders, P J Lord-Smith, Northwood Books

Construction contract law
Engineering Law and the ICE Contracts (4th Edn) M W Abrahamson, Applied Science Publishers
Hudson's Building and Engineering Contracts (10th Edn), I N Duncan Wallace, Sweet and Maxwell
Building and Civil Engineering Standard Forms, I N Duncan Wallace, Sweet and Maxwell
Building Contracts (4th Edn), D Keating, Sweet and Maxwell

Contract law in general
Cheshire and Fifoot's Law of Contract, M P Furmston, Butterworths

Law in general
The English Legal System, K J Eddey, Sweet and Maxwell
Osborn's Concise Law Dictionary (6th Edn), John Burke, Sweet and Maxwell

Index

Abrogation (of arbitration agreement) 13
absence (of a party) 45
acceptance 64, 65
admissibility 36
admitted 25
advice (legal) 21
advocate 35
affidavit 28, 34
affirmation 34, 40
agreed list (of documents) 27
agreements
    arbitration 7
    ad hoc 8
    exclusion 10
    formal 65
    in writing 7
    of figures and documents 29
amendment (of pleadings) 26, 31
appeal 1, 4, 6, 58
application
    for extension of time 15
    to High Court *see* High Court
apply, liberty to 31
appointment
    of arbitrator 8, 10, 18, SD/7, SD/8, SD/9, SD/10
    terms of 33
Arbitration Act 1950 3, 7, 8, 9, 10, 14, 15, Appendix B
    section 1 14, 19
    4 8, 13
    6 8
    10 8, 9, 14, 19, 21
    12 15, 28
    13 15
    14 15, 43
    15 15
    17 57
    18 15, 20, 21, 51, 54, 55, 58
    19 20, 51
    20 15
    21 3
    22 60, 61
    23 59, 61
    26 3, 50, 57
    32 7
Arbitration Act 1975 4, Appendix C
Arbitration Act 1979 3, 6, 7, 10, 14, 16, 44, 45, 58, Appendix D
    section 1 3, 46, 47, 58, 59
    2 4, 31, 47
    3 48, 58
    5 17
    6 9, 21
arbitrator
    advantages of 4
    definition of 1
    London Court of 9

INDEX 147

notice of 69, SD/3, SD/6
arbitrator
    authority of 23
    powers of 14
    qualifications of 70
    selection of 70
attendance (at hearing) 38
authority, appointing 20, 70
award 43, 44, SD/21
    costs of 56
    interim 44

Blanket denial 26
breach of contract 25, 47
Building Contract, Standard Form of 2, 7, 13
bundles of documents 41
burden of proof 37

Capacity, judicial 20
certificate, withholding of, by engineer 11, 12
charges, arbitrator's 20
Chartered Institute of Arbitrators 3, 9, 71
Civil Evidence Act 1968 33, 36
Civil Evidence Act 1972 33, 35
circumstantial evidence 33
claim, by contractor 67, 68
Claim, Points of 24, 25, 26, SD/12
Clause 12 (of ICE Conditions) 6, 11, 36, 47, 69, 70
Clause 66 (of ICE Conditions) 10, 11, 18, 21, 69, 72, SD/2
commencement of arbitration 11
Commercial Court 32, 59
common fund basis (of costs) 55
completion (of works) 11
confidentiality 6, 28, 68
consent 23, 31, 72
consent awards 49
consideration 62
consolidation 12
construction period 66
contemporaneous notes 37, 40
contract
    breach of 25
    constitution of 64, 65

law of 20
copies of documents 27, 34
costs 26, 32, 48, 49, 52, 75
    award of 5, 9, 15, 43, 51, 52, 53, 54
    bill of 24
    'follow the event' 52
    minimising 9
    of the award 20, 49, 51
    of the reference 49, 51
    taxation of 50, 54, 55
counsel 9, 24, 30, 37, 74
    'fit for' 24, 28
counterclaim 24, 52, 72
counter-offer 64
court proceedings, stay of 8, 13
credibility 5
cross-examination 34, 40, 41, 74

Damage: general damages; special damages 25
death (of arbitrator) 8, 10, 21
Defence, Points of 24, 25, SD/14
delay
    of arbitration proceedings 3, 6, 15, 20, 26, 72, 73
    of works 66, 73
Denning, Lord, Master of the Rolls 48, 49, 60, 69
deny 25
diary 37, 66
direct evidence 33
directions 24
    meeting for 23
    order for 23
discovery of documents 22, 26, 27, 28, 45, 63, 74
discretion of arbitrator 29
disruption 66
documentary evidence 33, 74
documents
    discovery of, see Discovery
    lists of 72, SD/19
    production of 14
'documents only' procedure 32, SD/10
Donaldson, Lord Justice v–vii, 45, 46

Economy (of costs) 5
enforcement, of awards 57
engineer's decision 11, 68
English law 2, 6, 22, 44
equity 49
errors, accidental 57
errors of law 12, 58
evidence 20, 33
Evidence Act 1938 33
evidence
    of fact 35
    proof of SD/20
    relevance of 36
examination-in-chief 40, 41
exclusion agreements 48, 58, 59
exclusion of right to appeal 7, 10
ex parte proceedings 16
expedition 5, 9
experts, appointment and role of 4, 5, 9, 22, 23, 35, 36
expert knowledge, arbitrator's use of 46, 47, 60
extension of time 31, 72, 73

Fact
    evidence of 33, 35
    findings of 45
    questions of 24, 46, 58
FCEC Form of Subcontract 7, 12, 13
FIDIC Form of Contract 7, 13, 18
figures as figures, agreement of 42
finality 6, 43, 58, 75
'fit for counsel' 24, 48
flexibility (of arbitration) 5
forewarning 24
freedom of choice (of arbitrator) 4
functus officio 57
Further and Better Particulars, *see* Particulars

Headings (in award) 44
hearing 22, 45
    adjournment of 39
    location of 30
    preparation for 74
    venue of 30
hearsay evidence 33, 36

High Court 3, 14, 15, 20, 28, 31, 34, 47, 57, 58, 59
    application to 4, 17, 19, 55
    appointment of arbitrator by 8, 9, 21
    judgment of 3, 57
hospitality (from a party) 31

ICC Rules 13
ICE Arbitration Procedure (1973) 10, 20
ICE Conditions of Contract 6, 7, 10, 12, 13, 18, 65 (*see also* Clause 12: Clause 66)
ICE List of Arbitrators 70
ICE, President of 10, 18, 19, 20, 70, SD/5
immediate arbitration 11, 12, 70
impartiality 19, 23, 30, 70
implied acceptance (of tender) 64
'in any event' 52, 73
incapacity (of arbitrator) 8, 10, 21
inspection of documents 27
intent, letters of 65
interest, award of 48
interest, in a party 19
interim award 43, 44, 53
interlocutory proceedings 16, 22, 30, 31, 45, 72
irrevocability of arbitrator's authority 14

JCT Form of Contract 2, 7, 13
judicial
    capacity 20, 70
    review 10
jurisdiction, challenges to 39

Law
    choice of 2
    compliance with 45
    English 1, 2, 3
    errors of 12, 58
    procedural, of arbitration 2
    proper, of contract 2
    questions of 10, 24, 31, 45, 47, 55, 58, 75

INDEX

Law Reform (Miscellaneous Provisions) Act 1934 48, 49
leading (a witness) 40, 41
legal advice 21, 47
letters of intent 65
liability 23, 43
liberty to apply 31
Limitation Acts 31, 47
lists of documents 72, SD/19
litigation 5
London (as venue for hearing) 30
London Court of Arbitration 9

Meeting, failure to attend 15, 16
method statement 63
misconduct 59, 60, 61
mistaken behaviour 60

Natural justice, rules of 61
New York Convention 4
notes, witness referring to 40
notice
    of arbitration 18, SD/3, SD/6
    to concur 13, 18, 21, SD/4, SD/6
notices, under contract 67

Oath, evidence on 34, 40, 74
obstructive party 9
offers
    open 53
    sealed 53
    to settle (effect on costs) 52, 75
Official Referee's Schedule *see* Scott Schedule
oncosts 64, 67
operative part of award 44, 45
opinion, evidence of 33, 35, 36
oral evidence 33, 34
orders 24, 45
Order for Directions 23, 72, SD/12
original documents 34

Particulars
    Further and Better 26, 73, SD/16, SD/17
    schedule of 25
party and party costs 55

payment into court 53
'Peremptory' 16
perjury 34
pleadings 15, 16, 22, 23, 24, 45, 72, 73, 74
    amendment of 26
Points of Claim, Defence, Reply *see* Claim, Defence, Reply
powers
    arbitrator's 14–17
    extension of 17
preliminary meeting 23, 30, 45, SD/11
preliminaries 22, 71, 74
preponderance of probability 37
president (of professional body) 4, 18, 19
prior knowledge (of matters in dispute) 19
pricing notes, contractor's 27, 63, 68
primary evidence 33
privacy 6, 38
privilege 27, 28, 74
procedural law 44
procedure 40, 45
programme of construction 63, 64, 66
progress charts 66
proof of evidence 37, SD/20
publication of award 50, SD/22
public policy 9

Qualification
    of arbitrator 19
    of a tender 64
quantum 23, 43, 68
Queen's Bench Division 32, 59
questions (by arbitrator) 41

Raymond, Sir Robert 1
real evidence 33, 35, 42
reasons (in award) 44, 45, 46, 47, 48, 59, 74
recitals 44, 45
records (during construction) 66
re-examination 40, 41

refusal
    to act 8, 10, 14, 19, 21
    to appoint 21
relevant documents 28
reluctant party 15, 20
remission to arbitrator 60, 61, 75
removal (of arbitrator) by court 10, 14, 59
replacement of arbitrator 14, 19
representation 5, 22, 23, 39
Reply, Points of 24, 25, SD/15
RIBA Form of Contract *see* JCT Form of Contract
RIBA, President of 13
Rules of the Supreme Court (RSC) 59

Scott Schedule 27, SD/18
sealed offer 53
secondary evidence 33
sequence (of hearing) 38, 42
setting aside (of award) 60, 61, 75
settlement, negotiated 49
single arbitrator 8
small claims 32, SD/9, SD/10
special case 3
specific performance 43, 44
Stamp Act 1891 34
Standard Form of Building Contract *see* JCT Form
standard of proof 37
stay (of court proceedings) 8, 13, SD/1

Subcontract, Form of *see* FCEC
subcontractor 12
subpoena 15, 34
surprise tactics 22

Tape recording of hearing 29, 42
tax and settle 20, 21, 54
taxation (of costs) 51, 54, 55, 56
telephone, communication by 31
tender 62, 63, 64, 65
third party notice 12
tort, law of 20
transcript of hearing 29, 42
tribunal, constitution of 8
trustee basis (of costs) 55
truth, ascertaining 27, 74
two-stage procedure (under ICE Conditions) 11, 13

United Nations Commission on International Trade Law (UNCITRAL) Rules 9

Vacancy, filling of 8, 10, 21
variations 28, 63, 66
varied quantity/type of work 63, 71

Withholding certificate 11, 12, 69
without prejudice 28, 53
witnesses 27, 30, 34, 37
witness's signature on award 44, 48
written evidence 9